Self

AN INTRODUCTION TO
PHILOSOPHICAL PSYCHOLOGY

This book is one of a series, Traditions in Philosophy, published by Pegasus in cooperation with Educational Resources Corporation, which has developed and created the series under the direction of Nicholas Capaldi, Professor of Philosophy, Queens College, New York.

Self

AN INTRODUCTION TO
PHILOSOPHICAL PSYCHOLOGY

Gerald E. Myers

PEGASUS   NEW YORK

Library of Congress Catalog Card Number 68-59624

PRE

To
Mary V. Myers
and
Harold W. Myers

Prefatory Note

The chapters of this book can be read as progressing from a discussion, in the first four chapters, of topics relevant to the concept of self, to considerations pertinent to the notion of self-control in Chapters Five through Seven, and to the subject of self-knowledge in the final three chapters. But it is throughout an essay about what we essentially need to know in order to know ourselves. It is offered as an example of philosophical psychology, or, if you prefer, of psychological philosophy.

G. E. M.

Contents

Prefatory Note vii

ONE ☐ Self 13
1. *The Philosophical Concept of the Self*
2. *Knowledge of the Self*
3. *Responses to Hume's Problem*
4. *Some Suggestions*

TWO ☐ Mental and Physical 29
1. *The Distinction*
2. *Mental and Physical Events*
3. *Difficulties*
4. *Autonomy of Mental Reports*
5. *Intentionality*
6. *The Identity Hypothesis*
7. *Pragmatics of the Issue*

THREE ☐ Three Claims about Experience 45
1. *Experience and Biophysics*
2. *Perceiving as Experiencing*
3. *Particular Experiences*

FOUR ☐ Thought 59
1. *Thinking*
2. *Naked Thought*
3. *Inner Speech*

FIVE ☐ Motivation 70
1. *Contemporary Research*
2. *Aggression*
3. *"Always a Cause"*
4. *Hidden Causes and Decision*

SIX ☐ Emotion and Feeling 88
1. *Some Theories*
2. *Emotions and Feelings*
3. *Knowing Our Feelings*

SEVEN ☐ Fantasy 102
1. *Imagination*
2. *Fantasy*
3. *Fantasies and Body-Image*
4. *Self and Body-Image*

EIGHT ☐ Memory 116
1. *Biology and Memory*
2. *Psychology and Memory*
3. *Philosophy and Memory*
4. *Memory and Retrospection*
5. *Memory and Self*

NINE ☐ Introspection 131
1. *Concepts of Introspection*
2. *Two Recent Introspective Studies*
3. *Introspection and Philosophy*

TEN ☐ Self-Knowledge 148

Notes 153

Supplementary Bibliography 167

Index 169

Self

AN INTRODUCTION TO
PHILOSOPHICAL PSYCHOLOGY

1

Self

His causes were air, and ether, and water, and many other strange things. I thought he was exactly like a man who should begin by saying that Socrates does all that he does by Mind, and who, when he tried to give a reason for each of my actions, should say, first, that I am sitting here now, because my body is composed of bones and muscles, and that the bones are hard and separated by joints, while the muscles can be tightened and loosened, and, together with the flesh and the skin which holds them together, cover the bones; and that therefore, when the bones are raised in their sockets, the relaxation and contraction of the muscles make it possible for me now to bend my limbs, and that is the cause of my sitting here with my legs bent. And in the same way he would go on to explain why I am talking to you: he would assign voice, and air, and hearing, and a thousand other things as causes; but he would quite forget to mention the real cause, which is that since the Athenians thought it right to condemn me, I have thought it right and just to sit here and to submit to whatever sentence they may think fit to impose. For, by the dog of Egypt, I think that these muscles and bones would long ago have been in Megara or Boeotia, prompted by their opinion of what is best, if I had not thought it better and more honorable to submit to whatever penalty the state inflicts, rather than escape by flight.

Plato's *Phaedo*

1. The Philosophical Concept of The Self

Socrates' point in the above epigraph may be put like this: It would be grotesque to say that his body decided to remain in prison and accept the death penalty; obviously, it was *he,* Socrates, who decided and was responsible for his sitting in the jail awaiting his end. Socrates' body was simply executing the orders of Socrates, the person or self housed in or somehow connected with that body. A person or self is certainly not identical with the body in which it lives, according to Socrates, since our bodies obviously do not ponder alternatives and make decisions; on the contrary, it is *we,* conceived as persons or selves somehow *more* or *other* than our bodies, who weigh and pick from among alternatives, manifesting our decisions in the way *we* move our bodies. Traditionally, that aspect or part of a person which ponders, decides, and initiates changes in that person's body has been known as "the self." What we mean by a "person" or "human being" must therefore include more than a human body; a human body is not a human being until a "self" has been added.

Another way of introducing the traditional concept of the self is to offer it as the claim that, for each of us, it is "oneself" rather than one's body which is referred to by the first-person pronoun; "I" refers only incidentally to my body, but it refers primarily and essentially to that other aspect of me which is "myself." It would be grotesque, on the traditional account, for you to tap some part of your body and insist that your use of "I" referred to *that;* it would be almost as absurd to suggest that "I" refers to the entire body rather than any part of it. If we were merely bodies, personal pronouns would be linguistic superfluities, but clearly they are not, since they refer to selves while *impersonal* pronouns in most languages refer to whatever is not a self or person. Thus, the problem of explicating the concept of the self is the problem of explaining what, for each of us, is the referent of the first-person pronoun.

A contemporary Socrates might cite recent experimental achievements on behalf of the claim that "I" must refer to something other than one's body, that other being *oneself.* The pertinent scientific achievement concerns amputees. An amputee, who had manipulated the conventional harness-operated arm for twenty-six years, has recently succeeded in using a new device, substituting for his amputated arm, for lifting things—in the language of the public announcement of the feat—"merely by thinking the lifting process." The new artificial limb has not been attached directly to the man but is connected to him via electrodes; these, attached to the stump of his upper arm, are also connected to a large computer which translates the signals with the flexing movements and stress control of the artificial limb. The novelty here is not the translation of electric signals into mechanical force but the translation into stress control. Former clamp-like devices required the same force, whether lifting a feather or a brick. The signals that tell the arm when to use the biceps and triceps muscles and when to exert stress were sorted out after several years of experimenting, and a mechanical arm was then built that translated the signal–information from the computer into flexing movements with a stress that can be controlled merely by "thinking it." The amputee, intending to grasp a feather rather than a brick, sends the appropriate electric signals as a result of his deliberate intention from the stump of his arm to the computer which conveys this information to the artificial limb, which then exerts only the force required to lift a feather. The amputee may say of the electric signals themselves, as Socrates said of the movements of his limbs, that they are what "*I* cause to happen." It is *oneself* who initiates the changes in the brain resulting in the electric signals sent to the muscular system; it is another case of the body responding to orders from the self whose body it is.

The self, then, is initially conceived as what is referred to by "I" when it is true to say "*I* caused such-and-such changes in my body." Given the beliefs that my body is not what is primarily or essentially meant by "I," and that I and not my body often cause changes in my body, and that the expression "my body" includes reference to all the physico-chemical events constituting my body, it is indeed natural to conclude, as many distinguished thinkers have concluded, that the *self* is a non-physical, nonchemical *something*. It is natural, upon such assumptions, to infer that what is essentially referred to by "I" is a *nonbodily something*. This conclusion is often expressed by saying that oneself is a mental, psychic, or spiritual thing or being. Certain philosophies and religions owe their appeal to the fact that this conclusion really does seem to their adherents to fit the facts.

It should be remarked that, according to some philosophers, the self is not only not identical with one's body, it is also not identical with one's mind. It can be argued that, just as specific changes in my bodily condition are caused by me rather than by my body, so particular changes in my mind or mental condition originate with me rather than in my mind. My mind is often as responsive as my body to what *I* decide to do, decide to think about, and so on. As my body is mine, so my mind is mine, leaving *me* in some sense the "possessor" of my mind and my body and not identical with either or both. It appears that Descartes (1596–1650) accepted this account. In considering what he should or should not believe in certain difficult cases, Descartes said that "it seems to me that it is the business of the mind alone, and not of the being composed of mind and body, to decide the truth of such matters."[1] This indicates that Descartes distinguished himself, conceived of as somehow composed of his mind and body, from both his mind and body. Descartes appears to have believed that, just as it was better for *him* to leave his respiratory system to breathe for itself, so it was sometimes expedient for *him* to abdicate and permit his mind to think for itself. If so, then the human being consists of a body, a mind, and a self. The self is, in some sense, the *possessor* of a mind and a body, and is what is referred to, by each of us, by the first-person pronoun. In particular, the self is what can initiate changes in the mind and body which it possesses. We may call this the "philosophical" concept of the self, to distinguish it from other concepts found in the literature of psychoanalysis, personality theory, and empirical psychology. The "philosophical self" has also been referred to in traditional philosophy as the pure ego, the unity of consciousness, the personal subject, and the soul. Whatever label used, the notion of the self is of something neither physical nor mental; rather, it "owns" a mind and a body and can set off changes in both possessions. To simplify the following discussion, and because it probably represents the philosophical problem most vividly, we shall focus on the self considered as a *nonbodily* something.

2. Knowledge of the Self

David Hume (1711–1776) expressed for many thinkers *the* perplexity about the philosopher's self: "There are some philosophers who imagine we are every moment intimately conscious of what we call our *self* . . . For my part, when I enter most intimately into what I call *myself,* I always stumble on some particular perception or other, of heat or cold, light or shade . . . I never can catch *myself* at any time without a perception, and never can observe anything but the perception."[2] Hume confessed that if someone else claimed to have any kind of "perception" of *himself,* he could not understand the claim and thus could no longer reason with such a thinker. Since he could not detect any single referent, of the sort required by the philosophical concept of the self, Hume concluded that selves or persons must be analyzed as "bundles" or "collections" of perceptions and experiences; selves are not "things" but series of perceptual experiences. It is worth noting that he subsequently acknowledged doubts about his official conclusion concerning the self, remarking that the whole topic is exceedingly baffling.[3] Hume's contribution was to emphasize how we think an experience of self ought to be possible, how we can feel on the very brink of coming upon it introspectively, and how we therefore feel highly disconcerted when no self is revealed to awareness. Our introspections disclose specific feelings, sensations, and perceptions, but nothing corresponding to the concept of self is detectable.

Hume showed how natural it is to expect to locate introspectively an elusive referent for "I" and how perplexing it is to experience the frustration of that expectation. He showed how the question "*What* am I?" is at once philosophically bewildering and psychoanalytically haunting. The question "*Who* am I?" unless amnesia has occurred, is easy to handle; one answers that by giving relevant autobiographical details. Similarly, "*What sort of person* am I?" is philosophically harmless; even though we may resort to tests and psychiatric assistance to find the answers, we do know in what directions to look for the answers. But the question "*What* am I?" is not a query about either my identity or my personality. I know, at this moment, that *I* am responsible for writing these words, and I know that I mean by "I" some sort of nonbodily and nonmental cause of what I'm doing now. There seems to be an I-at-this-moment which is responsible for my writing these words at this moment; in asking "*What* am I?" I'm asking what it would be like to apprehend this I-at-this-moment. I'm asking what features it would display to *self-awareness.* I know what a headache is by experiencing it, what sorrow is by experiencing it; similarly, it seems that I ought to know *myself* by experiencing it. Thus, when I end up like Hume, my query "What am I?" sums up my confusion. For in failing to find myself introspectively, I begin to wonder if the concept of myself as a nonbodily cause-at-this-moment of my present actions is possibly confused and mistaken, and then "*What* am I?" expresses no precise question but only general confusion. In any case, Hume's perplexity about the self seems to have resulted from his supposing that "What am I?" means "What would it be like to experience myself?" but then discovering the question to be seemingly unanswerable.

3. Responses to Hume's Problem

(A) An alternative to Hume's account is simply to deny his claim that the self cannot be experienced. Some theorists may agree with a contemporary psychologist who asserts that the self is a "kind of primitive experience about which communication is virtually impossible . . . one can experience the self but this experience must be uniquely personal . . . 'I am what I am' is the succinct Biblical assertion that selfhood cannot be further defined but must be experienced."[4]

The claim that one has experienced something that we might all expect to share but in fact do not, and toward which we cannot even be helped by a minimal description of the experience, is initially suspect. We may suppose that certain important, poignant experiences are reported as "experiences of selfhood" without assuming that they involve the direct awareness of the philosopher's self. Similarly, we may doubt that a person has ineffably experienced the divine, though confident that he alludes to an unusual experience that may be difficult to verbalize. But the difficulty for this alternative to Hume is even deeper. The problem is not so much to assess the probable truth or falsity of the claim that the self has been experienced; it is rather the problem of trying to make the claim *intelligible*.

In this respect, Hume's position is superior to the alternative being considered. We can understand how someone might set out to find an elusive something (in this case "the self") that is only indicated in minimal terms (in this case "the nonbodily cause of what I do") and discover that, given the minimal descriptive clue as to what one is seeking and the disappointing experiences during the quest, one's search had failed. But the case is different when, contradicting Hume, success is claimed. For we expect at least two communications from someone who has experienced *himself*: First, he should be capable, by virtue of his successful experience, of now adding to the originally meager description of what the self is; his experience should inform him further about the nature of himself. Secondly, he should be capable of indicating how others might secure for themselves a similar awareness of self, just as he might tell us that a remarkable experience of colors was the result of taking LSD. However, as we have seen, the claim that the experience of self occurs but is *ineffable* fails in both respects. Consequently, we really don't understand the claim, and to that extent it ceases to qualify as a persuasive alternative to Hume.

(B) One may agree with Hume that one's self is never disclosed to awareness but argue that its existence must nonetheless be *postulated.* On this view, we abandon hope of becoming self-aware, but we must assume the existence of the philosopher's self. Otherwise, how do we continue to respect Socrates' point? We are forced to believe in the existence of an imperceptible self. Otherwise, how do we explain the fact that some of our behavior is intentional and deliberate rather than reflex and capricious? Without reference to an *I,* this fact seems either to be not a fact or strangely unexplained. Sometimes, on this view, the postulated self is described not only as the *nonbodily cause* of certain changes in oneself, but also as "the unity of consciousness" and "that which is psychologically identical from moment to moment." The self gives unity to my experiences, such that I collect them all as *mine,* and it endures as *the same* in time, such that I consider myself, amid constant change, as somehow the same person today that I was yesterday.

A recurrent objection to this view is that the philosophical concept of the self is still too obscure to explain anything. It is illusory, therefore, to suppose that the postulated self can be used to explain how I behave, as postulated electrons can be used to explain how things happen in a cloud chamber. Many technical considerations can be marshaled to emphasize how "unscientific" is the concept of the self, how misleading, therefore, is the attempt to compare postulating it to postulation of unobservable events in physics. The theory of electrons involves certain predictions. But to the question, "What does the postulated self yield as predictions?" the only answer is "Nothing."

Another objection is that postulating the self neither meets nor appreciates the spirit of "*What* am I?" as it has been asked by Hume and so many others. For them, the question expresses wonderment about what it would be like to experience one's self, as well as perplexity about the seeming impossibility of any such experience. The situation, recall, is as follows: I am right now aware that *I,* something apparently not identical with my body, am right now writing these words, and I feel strongly that my vivid awareness that *I* am writing these words ought to be followed by an equally vivid awareness *of* that I. But that fails to occur, and I am left wondering *what* I am, what it would be like to be aware of the I that I know to be right now writing these words.

We need to appreciate this account of the occasion that prompts "*What* am I?" Otherwise, we don't understand why postulating a self seems so unsatisfactory and irrelevant. Nor would we appreciate why rival philosophical taxonomies of the self—as event, state, substance, function, relation, etc.—seem so beside the point. Whether *I* be an event or a substance, "*What* am I?" asks what it would be like for me to be aware of myself; the nature of a hypothetical experience is what haunts one here, not the philosophical labels of event, substance, etc. Moreover, unless the hypothetical experience of self-awareness occurs, one may conclude that, in postulating a self, one is merely showing one's determination to believe in something which one's experiences indicate to be non-existent. I eventually lose interest, however, in an I that I can't be aware of, and that is the plight of the postulated self.

(C) Philosophers, especially those in the Anglo-American tradition, have sometimes assumed that knowledge of an empirical statement must be based upon some observation, either introspective or perceptual. Knowing that I feel hot is based upon my introspectively observing how I feel, and knowing that you feel hot is established by observing your behavior and testimony. This assumption has been challenged recently, and it has been persuasively argued that counter-examples are easy to locate.[5] For instance, my knowledge that I intend to swim tonight or that I am now sitting is not really based upon any observation. This can be appreciated once you try to identify the observation upon which you might mistakenly think such knowledge is founded. For, surely, it would only be in a rare, odd situation that you would assert that you knew what you intended to do, or that you knew that you were walking, running, or sitting, because of some specific observation that you had made.

Thus, if "*How* do you know?" implies that there is either

a method or an observation involved, the question has no appropriate answer where what is known are one's own intentions or one's own activities (thinking, walking, etc.). All that one can do is to deny the question by declaring that one knows what one intends to do but not because of any observation. This contention does seem correct, and it might seem applicable to our problem about whether and how the self is known. It is not evident that any philosopher, distinguished or otherwise, has applied this concept of "knowledge without observation" to our topic, but if someone did, what should we say? What should we think if someone said, "I know, but without any observation, that *I* am the nonbodily cause of my action right now of writing these words"? Or if someone said, "I know that the philosopher's elusive referent for "I" exists, but it *cannot* be observed. What Hume did not realize is that you can know that you exist, as you know that you are walking, but without observing or being aware of yourself or your walking. Hume was correct in holding that one cannot be aware of the self, but he was wrong in his skepticism about its existence." How ought we respond to this?

Our observation, similar to that made about (A) above, is perhaps sufficient. Of course, (A) and (C) are quite different contentions; the former holds that I can know that I (in the philosophical sense) exist because I am *self*-aware, whereas the latter holds that, though I cannot be aware of what "I" refers to, yet I can "know without observation" that I exist. But the criticism of (C) is like that of (A); (A) opens the door to all sorts of "proofs" by appealing to what highly private, personal experiences are alleged to reveal, and (C) opens the door to all sorts of "proofs" by appealing to what can be known without having to observe or test. It is unnecessary to inquire here why I can know that I am sitting without making any observation. It is enough to note that sitting is a commonly shared activity, and we can therefore understand someone who says that he knows, without any observation, that he is sitting.

But a person claiming to know, without being aware of his self, that it nonetheless exists, hardly solves our problem. For we want to know *what* the self is, and our person can neither tell us, on the basis of his nonobservational knowledge, anything more than that the self is a nonbodily cause (which is just to reiterate the claim and not to substantiate it), nor even how he discovers that "I" does have as referent a nonbodily cause. That is, if I don't already know without observation that the philosophical "I" exists, or if I don't realize, upon reflection, that I possess such knowledge, then I really don't understand what our person is claiming. I have no idea of how to assess his claim. As noted previously, perhaps no thinker has argued that he in fact does know, without observation or special awareness, that *he* (in the required sense) exists. But if he did, the probability is that, like Hume, most of his audience would confess not to understand him nor know how to reason further with him.[6]

4. Some Suggestions

(A) Children are taught to substitute "I" for their names when talking about themselves. If a very young child is asked, after learning to use the first-person pronoun in appropriate contexts, whether his use of "I" refers just to his body or to something else, he will express bewilderment. For he did not learn, in acquiring the use of "I," that the pronoun does or does not refer to his body. Somewhat older, he draws a distinction between himself as owner and his body as owned; he calls his body, like his tricycle, *mine*. If he is then asked whether "I" refers to just his body or something else, he will probably express a more sophisticated bewilderment, characteristic of the burgeoning as well as the burgeoned philosopher, since he appreciates the logical fact that owner and owned can hardly be identical, yet also appreciates the realistic fact that there is only his body to point to as the referent of "I." The bewilderment thickens when he subsequently refers the responsibility for his actions to himself rather than to his body. He has learned to speculate like Socrates, like many of us. He is ripe for Hume's bewilderment.

The conclusion that one's self is a nonbodily something is drawn from the premisses that I am not identical with my body and that I can cause changes in my body. But part of the problem has its source in how we understand the word "body," and if we appreciated that fact we might then see how we can sensibly deny the premiss that I am not identical with my body; or, if not quite that, at least how we might deny the premiss that I am not identical with a bodily something. Most of us probably associate "the body" primarily with something publicly perceptible and only capable on its own of reflex behavior. Whether this is to be ungenerous toward our own bodies was a consideration of Spinoza (1632–1677) when he remarked, while noting the already-known "marvels" of the human body, "No one has so far determined what the body is capable of . . ." [7]

Substituting "organism" for "body" *can* work philosophical wonders. We are less resistant, if at all, to thinking of ourselves as physiological "organisms" than as "bodies," and for good reasons. The word "organism" was invented to refer to a physiological entity that is alive, self-moving, develops, evolves, is capable of feelings, thoughts, etc. which are not publicly perceptible, capable of a psychological dynamic, and so on. The word "body" does not connote so richly. For common-sense reasons we may not boggle, therefore, at identifying ourselves as organisms, at understanding the referent of "I" to be identical with the referent of "this organism." Indeed, just this simply, the puzzlement attending "*What* am I?" may be dissipated. Of course, I am not merely a body; *I* am this complex organism sitting here. And notice: Though we speak of "my body" and "your body," we don't speak of "my organism" and "your organism." In the vocabulary of bodies, owner and owned get distinguished, but not so in the vocabulary of organisms. The human organism has no landlord, being its own proprietor.

Certainly, some thinkers may object to our suggestion that the referent of "I" is not a nonbodily (and nonmental) something, that it is rather identical with "this organism sitting here, writing these words," etc. They may argue that this suggestion is theologically or scientifically incomplete, citing possible evidence, ranging from sacred scriptures to psychical research, for the conclusion that I am somehow "more" than a human organism. But many people are perplexed, like Hume, by and into the philosophical concept of the self, not because of very special or unusual evidence, but simply because of what routine experience seems to indicate. This suggestion is only intended for those who thought, on the basis of everyday experience, they could not identify *themselves* with their bodies, but consequently could not locate anything else with which to identify. It may suffice for those whose problem was, it turns out, a certain opinion about the human body.

(B) But citing the advantages of regarding persons as organisms rather than as bodies merely shows how "What am I?" can be answered, how a referent for the first-person pronoun, consistent with the way the pronoun was originally learned, is easily located. We must, in addition, suggest why this does not really conflict with anything revealed to our subjective experiences. For a person sharing Hume's perplexity may say, *"Objectively,* I know it makes sense to conclude that what *I* am is a certain type of organism. But, *subjectively,* I can't help returning to the feeling that what "I" refers to is more mysterious and elusive. I can't explain this feeling, but something in my experience must provoke it."

An explanation of this "returning feeling" is this: I slide into Hume's perplexity by thinking of myself as a *momentary cause,* as the cause of my writing these words at this moment. By accepting uncritically the premiss that I am not identical with my body, and given my knowledge that I am responsible for my writing these words at this very moment, I infer that "I" refers to the cause at this moment of my writing these words. I feel that this momentary cause, myself, ought to be discoverable, but it is not. The philosophical concept of the self is the concept of an elusive momentary causal agent.

The mistake here is to forget that the organism that I am *is* self-moving, capable of causing its own actions; it does not require another I to make it move. The source of this mistake is perhaps our inability to see, on the basis of what is revealed to subjective awareness, how we, as human organisms, move ourselves. Physiologists can explain how my muscles work when I write, but neither they nor I can apparently explain *how I originate* the action. I feel that I ought to be able to detect myself causing my own actions, ought to see how I originate my own movements. The absence of a supposed causal connection in the activity of the organism that I am leads me to fill the absence with a *nonbodily I as momentary cause* of a momentary action. In looking for the nonbodily I, I am looking for the missing cause in the organism's activity, but the nonbodily I turns out to be equally missing. But that frustrating fact does not prevent the "returning feeling," on the occasion when I say truly "*I* am the origin of this action," that the elusive cause in myself as an organism must therefore be "outside" myself as an organism, i.e., must be a nonbodily self or cause.

But in wondering *how* I originate my own actions, I have already committed the mistake of thinking that initiating an action is a causal process. Originating one's own action, however, is just *doing* it on one's own. Of course, the neurophysiological details of how I move my arm in writing these words are complex; they reveal, for example, the now familiar fact that, in writing, I originate changes in the brain and the nervous system that precede my arm movements. But there is no causal mechanism whereby I originate the initial item in the causal series leading to my arm movements, which is what I mistakenly assume in wondering "how" I initiate it. Of course, unlike lower forms of life, humans often plan, ponder, and deliberate before acting, and we sometimes mean to refer to that preparatory mental activity in speaking of "how" the act was done. But when, after the pondering and deliberating, I originate an action, there is no process whereby the organism that I am originates the action; originating the action is simply doing it on one's own. There is no more a special problem of "how" humans originate their actions than there is of how animals move themselves. Once I realize that there is no basis for "How do I originate my own actions?" and consequently am not tempted to think that "I" refers to an origin (other than the organism that I am) of my actions, the "returning feeling" that "I" *must* refer to a nonbodily and nonmental self may never return again.

(C) The concept of self is prominent in psychological and psychiatric literature.[8] Sometimes the philosophical concept of self seems to be defended, when, for example, it is said that effective therapy requires one's "experiencing" one's real self. It is sometimes suggested that mental health and self-knowledge depend upon literally experiencing one's self as one experiences, say, a feeling of hope or a sense of despair. However, clinical psychology, like experimental or behavioral psychology, generally avoids the metaphysical "I." What is rather intended by "self" is either the whole human organism, or the attitudes which a person has toward himself (his "image" of himself), or a set of distinctive processes (for instance, defense mechanisms) invoked by psychoanalytic theory to explain certain kinds of behavior.[9]

When clinical psychology stresses the importance of "the self," it means to emphasize how our ability to function depends upon our attitudes toward ourselves, and how such attitudes result from distinctive psychological as well as physiological processes. Understanding what are our attitudes toward ourselves (and others) and what produced them is a complex process which, if successful, constitutes self-knowledge. In this process we may experience "sudden insights" concerning our attitudes and their origins, but this does not imply that self-knowledge is ever the result of experiencing the sort of thing Hume vainly sought. Further, from a psychoanalytic perspective, it may be deleterious to suppose that self-knowldge can be acquired through a sudden, illuminating experience of one's elusive "real self" rather than through the complex process of understanding how the organism that one is has developed from infancy as it did.

In fact, it is startling to learn how complex are the conditions to be fulfilled if a child is to acquire, or retain, or acknowledge a sense of self. Studies of autistic children, withdrawn into their fantasy worlds, reveal that being able to use "I" in a normal way is hardly automatic.[10] Examples of eight- and nine-year-old youngsters who don't refer to themselves at all, or who may refer to themselves and others by "you," or refer to themselves by a mathematical formula and avoid pronouns altogether, or refer to themselves as machines or animals, point to many lessons. But two of these deserve mention here. First, recent investigations greatly reinforce the picture of the infant as a striving and demanding organism. How it fares in those first days, how its first movements get responded to, may figure significantly in shaping the subsequent psychology of that infant. The *psychological* demands, as it were, of the infantile organism are there long before it can become aware of them. Autistic children, who were rejected or ill treated as infants, are often found to be full of hatred and longing, hatred of a rejecting environment and longing for an accepting one. The infant's responses to rejection or acceptance may be such as to be describable as a young organism's refusal or inability to develop a sense of self.

Secondly, there is some evidence for the hypothesis that, if a child is to learn the normal uses of "I," he must experience more than love, affection, and warmth. Included also must be the realization that he *causally* operates upon his environment, that his wishes and volitions create changes in his world. People respond and objects move at his bidding. Deprived of this realization, the infantile organism may "give up" and withdraw autistically. And, at eight or nine years, a long, agonizing process of rehabilitation of that same organism may be required (if at all possible) before it can become a person, before it can handle personal pronouns in a normal way. Put in this light, the story of the human self is really a story of how the human organism acquires and modifies crucial attitudes toward itself. Becoming philosophically accurate about the origin and nature of the philosophical concept of the self is itself probably an important modification in attitude for many in securing a more accurate knowledge of who and what they are.

2

Mental and Physical

1. The Distinction

It is often asserted that the organism that I am is both
"mental" and "physical." Insofar as I have a mind, am rational
and think, I am a mental as well as a physical being. Also,
to the extent that I *feel,* in addition to behaving, I am a mental
creature. Psychology originated as the "mental science," as the
only discipline to study man as a mental being. Psychology,
unlike the physical sciences, aimed at understanding man as
the being that thinks and feels. The physics, chemistry, physiology, and anthropology of the human organism were, on this
view, outside professional psychology.

Before psychology separated from philosophy, attempts were
made to explain in theory certain prescientific ways of distinguishing the mental from the physical in everyday life and
discourse. Descartes' dualism between mind as one kind of
substance and the body as another kind is a case in point. A
thing (object, substance, stuff) *is* a combination of functional
and structural properties. When people referred to swords and
saddles as "physical," they alluded to the fact that swords and
saddles are things occupying three spatial dimensions (extended
in space), are composed of parts, and have distinctive causal

properties (can be used for distinctive functions). Assuming that a person *thinks* by virtue of having a *mind* or *soul* and not by virtue of having a body, then what is a mind or soul? Descartes' answer was that, like physical things, the mind is also a thing having distinctive causal properties (being able to think and, by so doing, to cause changes in its associated body). But unlike physical things, minds are not extended in space and do not have parts. Their structure is indivisible, "unitary and entire." [1] Moreover, according to Descartes, the mind and body of a person must be conceived, for everyday reasons, as interacting causally. If my brain is stimulated in a certain way, that stimulates my mind to think something, and the process works in reverse. Descartes even suggested the *place* of interaction, the pineal gland, a small glandular organ in the midbrain. He chose it as the link between mind and body because of its curious anatomical structure and because it seemed to have no assignable alternative function. [2]

Descartes' dualism appears to have won more rejection than acceptance, and this is probably due less to what philosophers call "technical" reasons than to the decline of theology as a supervisory spirit in philosophy and psychology. To be sure, Cartesian dualism is still a dominant feature of Western culture, but not of professional philosophy and psychology. The professionals have argued that they do not understand how anyone could know that he had a mind–substance of Descartes' description, or how even to understand the concept of a substance that is not in space and has no apparent structure and can only be asserted to be that which thinks. For it is obviously no help, when the question is "What is the nature of the mind which thinks?" to repeat "It is that which thinks." But, critics insist, that is all we get as an answer from Cartesian dualism. Finally, critics question the value of the view, even if its intelligibility is conceded. We learn about thinking and feeling, they argue, from biology and physiology, not from studies of supposed immaterial substances.

It has also been argued, on the other side, that Descartes found his proper heir in Freud. For what is psychoanalytic theory but the attempt to formulate the "structure" of the human mind? What has fascinated some about psychoanalysis *as theory* is its wealth of statement of *how* and *why* the mind works as it does. As the concepts of the theory accumulated—id, ego, superego, repression, transference, displacement, preconscious, unconscious, etc.—the mysteries of the mind's structure seemed to many to have at last been revealed. Freud said that his life had been devoted to explaining the dynamics between id (instinct), ego (the self adjusting to the environment), and superego (acquired conscience). But he also conjectured that future biology might replace psychoanalytic theory. Many of those continuing Freud's work retain his biological orientation, regarding psychoanalytic theory as antithetical to Cartesian dualism. Psychoanalytic theory, they argue, explains certain features of the developing biological organism that man is, not how a nonbiological mind interacts with a biological brain.

The relation of Freudianism to Cartesianism is one of the untold stories of our time. Until that is done, the philosophy of psychology will be in suspense about final judgment on the mental–physical distinction. The most that can be said is that Freudianism *may* be today's enrichment of Cartesianism, but certainly not all Freudians think so.

2. Mental and Physical Events

Professional philosophy has lost interest in the concept of the mind as a thing or substance. But philosophers still debate whether there are mental as well as physical *events*.[3] The procedure usually followed is this: Certain kinds of events typically labeled "mental" are examined for properties which will reveal them and certain other kinds of events typically labeled "physical" to be mutually exclusive. Feelings, dreams, and hallucinations are often selected as examples of what people call "mental." It is then asked whether what is meant, say, in typically labeling the running of rabbits or the acceleration of automobiles as "physical," is such that *no* event can be both mental and physical. Are there differences between the feeling of sorrow and the scampering of a rabbit which justify, not only the initial designations of the former as "mental" and the latter as "physical," but also the conclusion that nothing can be both mental and physical?

A familiar response to this question is to say that a rabbit's running, like any *physical* event, is (a) publicly perceptible, (b) in public space, and (c) an event about which perceptual reports *can* be erroneous. But a feeling of sorrow is (a′) necessarily private to one person's awareness, (b′) not in public space and perhaps not in space at all, and (c′) an event about which one's report *cannot* be mistaken. Thus, any event fitting (a′) – (c′) is, like a feeling of sorrow, mental; any event fitting (a) – (c) is, like a rabbit's running, physical; and, given these definitions, it clearly follows that nothing can be both mental and physical. There can be no doubt of course that there *are* both mental and physical events, since obviously there are feelings of sorrow and runnings of rabbits.

3. Difficulties

The first of several important objections to the thesis just described simply denies (a′) – (c′). There seems to be no contradiction in the conjecture that you and I *could* be simultaneously *aware* of my feeling of sorrow. We cannot describe *how* this could happen, but that is no objection, since we cannot, in fact, describe *how* you are aware of your sorrow or I of mine. If, however, you and I repeatedly reported sorrow simultaneously under the same conditions, this remarkable fact could lead us to conclude that we were unusual in sharing the same sorrow. If this were conceded, but the point then offered that you could not *have* my sorrow even though you might be co-conscious of it, the reply could be made that it may be true that, in some sense, if a feeling is yours, then it cannot be mine. But this fact will not distinguish the mental from the physical, since the same point holds for certain physical events. My frowning and laughing are physical events; yet, since you cannot frown my frown nor laugh my laugh, there is this respect in which my physical frowning and laughing cannot also be yours. Hence, this brand of "privacy" will not distinguish the mental from the physical such that no event can be both.[4]

Concerning (b'), how is its alleged truth known? Given that one's feeling of sorrow is not *felt* to be in any part of space, in no particular part of one's body, that does not by itself preclude its *being* in the brain or some other part of the body. How does one choose between locating a feeling of sorrow somewhere or not locating it anywhere? The problem apparently exists for (b) and physical events also. According to quantum mechanics, events cannot always be located exactly in space; if it makes sense to say of a physical event studied by physics that it "occurs *more or less* in *that* region of space," then it makes sense to say of a feeling of sorrow that it "occurs *more or less* in *that* region of space" (*e.g.,* that region of space occupied by the body of the sorrowful person), even though it cannot, on the basis of how it feels, be assigned any exact spatial location. Likewise, the sun's gravitational attraction on earth is a physical process, but how can one assign it a spatial location?[5] Accordingly, unassignability of spatial location does not appear to support the philosophical distinction between mental and physical events.

Debates about (c) and (c') are more subtle and more difficult to collect into a single issue, but, for many, it is this: Can one be mistaken in reporting "I feel sad," and can "I feel sad" be overridden or corrected by someone else? If not, and assuming that reports about physical events are always fallible, we should have a criterion for distinguishing mental and physical occurrences.

Suppose Jones claims that he was mistaken in sincerely reporting that he felt sad. The philosopher adhering to the doctrine that sincere reports of this sort must be infallible, must accuse Jones of irrationality or of not understanding expressions like "feeling of sadness." Jones must either be out of his mind or be ignorant of how words like "sad" are used. But suppose Jones protests that he was neither insane nor linguistically confused, and further that he offers evidence in behalf of his protests. Is it not arbitrary of the philosopher to insist that "I feel sad" is infallible? The philosopher may say, "I do not see *how* one can misjudge whether one feels sad or not." But Jones does not pretend to know *how* he made such a mistake; in such cases, there is no psychological machinery whose quirks can be detected. All he knows is that he wrongly believed that he felt sad. It does seem that Jones's claims is as convincing as the philosopher's, and, if so, the thesis that reports of mental events are incorrigible will not provide a criterion for distinguishing mental and physical events.

4. *Autonomy of Mental Reports*

A modified thesis, claiming less than infallibility for reports of mental states, is sometimes offered. This holds that, though Jones may err in reporting that he feels sad, the fact remains that *his* testimony about his own moods is the ultimate court of appeal. *Only he* can decide whether his reports of his own mental states are accurate or not. A person, according to this modified thesis, is the final judge about the accuracy of his reports about his own mental states; but he is never the final judge about the correctness of his reports about physical events, including his own bodily states. Speculations about superscientific instruments, telepathy, clairvoyance, and so on, must all acknowledge that, if Jones confidently and finally declares that he feels sad, then no conceivable instrument and no conceivable experience of someone else can contradict Jones's report. He and only he is the final arbiter; or, as the point is sometimes stated, first-person reports of mental states are autonomous.[6]

This view wants to maintain both that first-person reports of mental states are autonomous and that no other person or thing can ever override a first-person report. But suppose that Jones says sincerely at t_1 "I feel sad" and says also sincerely at t_2 "I remember now that I was mistaken in asserting that I felt sad at t_1." How is he to resolve the conflict between his two first-person reports, a conflict which can cause him to doubt the autonomy of all first-person reports in the present tense? To resolve it, he may turn to the testimony of others, records, etc. If so, then his first-person report is not autonomous, and "autonomy" is not a criterion of mental reporting.

A more serious problem is this: Suppose Jones says sincerely at t_1 "I think I feel sad, but I am not sure." Since this first-person report is autonomous, according to the view in question, it cannot be denied. But suppose further that Jones believes in the accuracy of a remarkable invention, a brain gadget which measures a person's moods; it is also especially adept at recognizing the immediate aftereffects of the presence or absence of sadness. So Jones attaches himself to the gadget and, on the basis of what the gadget indicates, decides whether he felt sad or not at t_1. The point is this: Jones says at t_1 that he is unsure whether he feels sad, though he thinks he is, and he is also certain that the assertion "I do feel sad at t_1," of which he is uncertain, is either true or false; he is inclined to think it true. Given Jones's autonomous report of doubt and his evidence of the brain gadget's efficiency, he is surely entitled to permit the gadget to decide whether the first-person report "I do feel sad at t_1" is true or false. If so, autonomy of first-person psychological reports is not a criterion of mental reporting.[7]

5. Intentionality

Some philosophers have revived the concept of *intentionality* for distinguishing the mental and physical.[8] They sometimes assert that mental *states* have the property of intentionality, but physical states never have it. Consider belief and fear as examples of mental states. It is said that when you believe or fear, you believe or fear something. States of belief and fear "refer to" or "intend" something, and it is such "referring to" or "intending" that is meant by "intentionality." If I now believe that Jones is hot; and you now believe that Smith is cold, our states are alike in both being beliefs but are different in what they "intend" or "refer to"; they differ in their specific intentionality. Moreover, in some cases, what my beliefs or fears relate to by "intending" or "referring" need not exist—for example, when I believe (or fear) that witcheš are marching on Washington. Now consider any physical state, it is said, and you quickly realize that the feature of intentionality (of "referring to" or "intending" something) could never characterize a physical state.[9]

One response to this view is to accept intentionality as a criterion marking off *some* mental states from *all* physical ones. Fear *can* be contrasted to all physical states by its displaying the feature of intentionality. But there are other emotional or mental states which fail to exhibit the feature. Anxiety is often cited as an example; one can be anxious without one's anxiety "referring to" or "intending" any specific something, whereas fear always has a specific object (whether existent or not). But in certain anxieties, it is claimed, the anxious person is in a turbulent state but unable to identify a specific something which the anxiety refers to, intends, or is about. Other mental states are held to be like anxiety in this respect, so that, at best, intentionality is a criterion for identifying *some* mental states.

Another response is to deny that belief and fear are states or episodes. Instead, they are held to be dispositions to behave in certain ways. My believing that you like me is not an occurrence at all, it is argued, but is rather my being "set" to act in a friendly way toward you, to speak well of you, etc. Similarly, fear is not merely a feeling or occurrence; it is being "set" to run, to strike out, to be paralyzed, etc., and unless one were so disposed to respond one would not really be afraid. Thus, those mental states alleged to have the distinctive feature of intentionality are now argued not to be states at all but are dispositions-to-behave instead.[10]

But this thesis, sometimes called behaviorism, creates its own difficulties. Perhaps the most important of them is that to analyze my believing that you like me, for instance, as just being "set" to *behave* in certain ways, is necessarily false because overly simple. It is too simple to say merely, if I believe that you like me, that I shall behave toward you in friendly fashion; I shall only *do* that, *if* I *want* to be friendly, *if* I *believe* there is any point in doing so, *if* I *hope* to gain something for both of us by doing so, and so on. That is, belief and fear cannot be analyzed simply as dispositions-to-behave; they must also be characterized in relation to *other* states or dispositions of wanting, believing, hoping, etc.[11]

This defect in an overly simple behaviorism has been cited in a recent and influential defense of intentionality as a limited criterion of the mental.[12] This current argument for intentionality refutes the too-simple behavioristic description of even *elementary* human behavior. Consider, for example, something as elementary as Jones's looking for his car. We cannot fully explain what is meant by his "looking for" his car by mentioning only Jones's overt behavior and dispositions to behave in certain ways. We must also mention that he will behave in certain ways, *provided* that he also wants, hopes, believes, etc. certain things. If these conditions did not hold, we should retract our assertion that Jones is really looking for his car. Assertions about a person's wanting, believing, hoping, etc. can all be characterized as "intentional" (in a manner reminiscent of our previous description of intentionality), in the sense that "I believe (hope, want, etc.) that A is B" can be true even though A is not B. But assertions about pushing, accelerating, exploding, etc. (physical states) are "nonintentional," in the sense that "I push or accelerate A up B" cannot be true unless A moves up B. According to this current argument, we revive the criterion of intentionality, as distinguishing the mental from the physical, by demonstrating that not even elementary human behavior, like looking for something, can be described solely in nonintentional assertions.

But this conclusion needs a second look. This current argument for intentionality does show that concepts, traditionally considered mental, like those of belief, want, hope, etc. can be collected together by reference to a feature reminiscent of what we have called intentionality. It does show, further, that elementary human *behavior* cannot be exclusively described by what are traditionally called physical concepts, like those of push, accelerate, explode, and so on. But the argument does *not* show that there are "mental states" in a traditional sense of this expression.

Traditional views held that we can introspectively identify our own mental states of believing, etc. and also discover that intentionality is a property of such states. But the *current* argument does not conceive of intentionality as a property of states but as a property of certain types of behavior. It does not try to establish the existence of mental states, which can be shown to be intentional such that they cannot also be physical. It does not really claim that the organism that I am is capable of being in mental states to which *only* mental concepts apply.

The current argument for intentionality, it appears, is compatible with the view that *all* the behavior and states of the organism that I am are, in some respect or other, physical or physiological. And some of this *behavior* and some of these states are also undeniably "intentional," in the special sense described.

6. The Identity Hypothesis[13]

The identity hypothesis, subject of many contemporary debates, holds that there are mental states but that they are *identical* with physical states. There are mental states, insofar as there are states which we are acquainted with in ourselves, like hoping, fearing, and paying attention to things, and these states, so far as our observational powers are concerned, are not in space and not publicly perceptible but only privately knowable. So far as our observational capacities can determine, there are "mental states" in the traditional sense of this expression. I can know now that I am paying attention to this sheet of paper and that doing so is responsible for my seeing the paper more distinctly, but the state of paying attention is not at all like a physical activity. Unlike physical states, it is neither observed nor inferred, yet I know it occurs as part of my experience. So ordinary experience supports the traditional view that mental states occur.

But the identity hypothesis proceeds to equate these mental

states with physical states, states in the brain. My fearing you is made identical, on this hypothesis, with one of my brain-states, on the grounds that what occurs in my brain is a necessary and sufficient condition of my fearing you, and that this brain-condition is *temporally simultaneous* with my experience of fearing you. The brain-condition is so "close" causally and temporally to my fear-state that it is naturally tempting to merge the two into one.

Highly sophisticated, technical discussions of the identity hypothesis have assumed that it is an intelligible conjecture. They assume that we can understand how the conjecture might be true. It is this assumption which will be briefly challenged here. Two sorts of explanations have been presented in current literature to show that the identity hypothesis is intelligible. The first holds that two different descriptions may in fact refer to one and the same thing, as is the case, for example, of "the husband of Xantippe" and "the teacher of Plato." It is an historical fact that both descriptions refer to Socrates. Likewise, it is argued by the identity hypothesis, the two descriptions "my fearing you" and "electrical pattern P occurring in my brain" may really refer to one and the same event.

But the problem confronting the identity theory is how to distinguish the cases where two or more descriptions *can* refer to the same phenomenon from those cases where two or more descriptions *cannot* refer to the same thing. For instance, "the man presently in front of me" and "the man presently behind me" cannot refer to the same man. Now how do we decide whether "my fearing you" and "electrical pattern P occurring in my brain" *can* or *cannot* refer to the same event or state?

The difficulty with the identity theory, thus far considered, is that it cannot help us to answer this crucial question. Thus far, the theory fails to specify any theoretical procedure by which we could discover whether or not "my fearing you" and "electrical pattern P occurring in my brain" refer to the same thing. Until this is achieved, it may be argued that the theory is really unintelligible. A special difficulty may prohibit any such achievement. Whenever two descriptions are discovered to apply to one and the same thing, it must be the case that that thing is identifiable via a third description that is logically distinct from the two which are coreferential. For example, it must be possible to identify the man referred to by "the President of the United States" and "the husband of Pat Nixon" *also* by "that man standing on the White House lawn," or by "that man on the television screen," etc. That is, it must be possible to indicate, without using the coreferential descriptions, what the thing is to which they both refer. But it seems *impossible* to do this in the case of "my fearing you" and "electrical pattern P occurring in my brain." One cannot refer to an event under the description "that event $\emptyset$" (where "$\emptyset$" is logically distinct from "my fearing you" and "electrical pattern P occurring in my brain") such that it may be discovered that the three descriptions are in fact all coreferential. Thus, the claim that my fearing you is identical with a brain-state seems unintelligible, for the reason that there is no way of specifying *the* event to which the two descriptions are alleged to refer. Yet what the identity theory claims is that there is something which is *the* event to which the descriptions both apply.

The second sort of explanation attempts to supply the identity hypothesis with a theoretical procedure by which my fearing you *can* be identified with my brain-state. It may argue that, as my skin is identifiable with the cells which *constitute* it, so my fearing you is identifiable with my brain-state as *constituting* it. But the problem is to make this claim intelligible. It is not clear that it makes sense to treat my fearing you as a complex thing like my skin. In any case, if my fearing you is to be conceived as a complex of constituent ingredients, then some procedure must be specified for analyzing the complex into its constituents. But no one seems able even to begin to do this in the case of my fearing you. How could you possibly embark upon such an analysis?

The other way in which the identity theory attempts to meet this challenge is to claim that my fearing you *is* a brain-state in the sense in which lightning *is* an electrical discharge (as defined by physics).[14] But the problem here is to show that one is not committing the genetic fallacy of identifying an effect with its cause. In seeing lightning what we see is a *flash*. That flash may be *caused* by a process which the physicist defines as an electrical discharge, but, it may be argued, that process as described by the physicist is postulated but not observed. But what could be meant by asserting that the *observed lightning* (the flash) is *identical with* an electrical discharge? Physics does not offer any help in answering this question; no science offers any theoretical procedure by which such identity could be confirmed or not. Thus, science does *not* appear to provide an analogy in terms of which we can understand what is asserted in making my fearing you identical with my brain-state. If the neurons in my brain fire in a certain way, that may indeed *cause* me to fear you, but what could possibly support the claim that my fearing you is the *same* phenomenon as the firing of my brain's neurons? Again, the problem for the identity hypothesis is to make itself intelligible, to *show how* it is that where there appear to be *two* phenomena there might in fact be only one.

Though the conclusion here is that the identity theory of mental and physical events is unintelligible in its attempt to show how two apparent phenomena are really one, this does not conflict with our previous denial of the philosophical distinction between the mental and the physical. To say that my fearing you cannot be intelligibly equated with my brain-state is not to insist upon any particular distinction between the mental and physical; it is simply to remind that when there are two things they cannot be one. But, as the next section will make explicit, this does not imply that my fearing you and my brain-states must be philosophically contrasted as mental and physical.

7. Pragmatics of the Issue

The argument of this chapter is that the *philosophical* contrast of mental and physical is valueless.[15] Every day, specific distinctions between mental and physical are, however, as appropriate as they have ever been. In one context, "mental" means "illusory" as in the case of hallucination. Or it may mean "abnormally caused in the absence of the normal physical cause"; when, for instance, we call the symptoms of hypochondriacs merely mental. Other meanings may be suggested. But the point is that these prephilosophical ways of contrasting the mental and the physical have developed somewhat haphazardly and somewhat independently of each other. Accordingly, there is no one underlying way of making the distinction; there are just these various contextual contrasts. If one starts with the actual usages of "mental" and "physical," one looks in vain for an underlying unity of distinction. For instance, a mirage may be called *mental* in the sense of being an illusion but be argued to be *physical* in the sense of being publicly perceptible. This example is typical, exhibiting the futility of seeking a philosophical distinction. Traditionally, the philosophical effort to contrast the mental and physical has been the attempt to show how, if an event is mental and not physical according to one existing method of distinction, then it is mental and not physical according to all the other important established ways of drawing the distinction. To say that the philosophical contrasting of mental and physical is valueless is just to say that this traditional philosophical effort, for the reasons given, has no chance of success.

It is probably true that, for some thinkers, it is pragmatically important whether a philosophical distinction between the mental and the physical can be drawn or not. For them, a systematic distinction supports other systematic distinctions of practical significance. They believe that if a criterion can be found for distinguishing mental phenomena from physical ones, then a theoretical basis exists for certain conclusions involving other alleged sharp distinctions. They may conclude, for instance, that if a symptom is classified as mental, then it must be removed or preserved through mental causation; or if it is diagnosed as physical, then it is to be treated via physical techniques. It might be inferred, accordingly, that if a person's headache is merely mental, without any normal physical basis, the way to remove it is through an act of will, by a grim resolve. If, on the other hand, the headache has a physical basis, then only surgery, drugs, etc. can serve to dissipate it. Or it might be inferred that only if one thinks of oneself as being a *mental something*, different from but potentially in control of the organism that one is, can one achieve such things as finding life meaningful, remaining energetic, overcoming anxiety, learning to love, and so on. Such results might be thought to depend, so to speak, upon one's psychologically stepping outside oneself as a physiological organism.

Suppose that, in some obscure way, a philosophical distinction between the mental and physical does seem to support such inferences. Perhaps, on the other hand, evidence of an everyday kind ought always to have shown such conclusions to be *unwarranted*. In any event, we certainly appreciate that fact nowadays. Merely classifying a symptom, effect, or achievement as "mental" or "physical" reveals nothing about its particular etiology or the causal techniques appropriate to it. Only by experiment do we find what can cause what. Thus, we learn now that people can eliminate the pain of angina pectoris by simply pushing a button; the button works a radio transmitter that energizes an electronic system under the skin, which in turn stimulates the carotid sinus nerves, and the pain quickly ceases. It is reported that composing or listening to poetry is therapeutic for some emotionally disturbed people; one authority is quoted as saying that poetry "really appeals to your nervous system." We hear of a physician reported to have shot fear into normal rats by injecting them with material from the brains of rats trained to be fearful. Evidence now exists for the conclusion that a baby's I.Q. is sometimes a result of the mother's diet during pregnancy. Recent investigations indicate that an excess of globulin in the blood may cause the changes in the brain nerve cells responsible for some forms of schizophrenia.

An experiment reveals that 19 out of 40 persons suffering from chronic asthma were provoked into asthmatic attacks by deceiving them into believing that they were breathing in pollen, indicating that this disease may have an attitudinal or emotional basis. New evidence supports the hypothesis that cancer may be connected with emotional stress which is not allowed outlet, which is prohibited from outward discharge by severe repression. It has been demonstrated that the knee jerk reflex can be reduced by as much as 67 per cent within four minutes of smoking a high-nicotine cigarette. Another recent study reports that about 80 per cent of 191 patients suffering from cardiovascular diseases, arthritis, cancer, diabetes, nervous disorders, and other diseases, had experienced a feeling of "giving up," at the time the physical illness attacked, in response to the loss of someone or something dear to them. This naturally indicates the hypothesis that an astonishing variety of physical illnesses can be triggered by the feeling or attitude known as "giving up." The hypothesis is not of course new, and maybe one heard it first from one's grandmother, but it is highly important to learn what actual evidence exists for it.[16]

These experimental investigations show that the psychological and physiological states of the organism that I am do not fit into a simple conceptual scheme. Learning which states cause which states does not require a scheme which carefully divides those states into mental and physical. If, for example, a person's depression is found to be "mental" (in the sense of having no identifiable bodily cause), a function of his attitude rather than of his body, it remains an experimental problem to find the proper remedy. In some cases the therapist's couch will suffice, in others drugs or shock treatment will be needed. Experimental investigations remind us, then, of the diverse and complex ways in which the states of the human organism interact. No neat causal scheme depicting the relations between those states is available. Accordingly, a philosophical attempt to contrast the mental and physical is not required to support any such scheme, is not in fact pragmatically significant.

3

Three Claims
about Experience

Human beings are conscious, have experiences. Some thinkers consider our discussion of the mental–physical distinction incomplete without an account of this obvious fact, because they say that being conscious or having an experience is certainly not physical. Some writers have said that experiences are puzzling, since they cannot be regarded as parts of the physical or physiological world. Experiences are puzzling for a second reason, others claim, because experiences are not susceptible to description. For example, I can describe the rainbow that I see, but I cannot describe my experience of seeing it. Thirdly, though we do indeed talk of our having "particular" experiences, the concept of a particular experience is not nearly so clear as the concept of a particular apple; the concept, until clarified, further adds to the confusion about what it is to be conscious or to have an experience. We move to a consideration of these three contentions.

1. Experience and Biophysics

Sir Charles Sherrington has eloquently expressed what, for

many, is the scientifically curious fact about being conscious or having an experience. Experiencing, he says, falls outside the energy-scheme of physics and neurophysiology.

> But, as to our *seeing* the star it [the energy-scheme of physics and neurophysiology] says nothing. That to our perception it is bright, has direction, has distance, that the image at the bottom of the eye-ball turns into a star overhead, a star moreover that does not move though we and our eyes as we move carry the image with us, and finally that it is the thing a star, endorsed by our cognition, about all this the energy-scheme has nothing to report. The energy-scheme deals with the star as one of the objects observable by us; as to the perceiving of it by the mind the scheme puts its finger to its lip and is silent. It may be said to bring us to the threshold of the act of perceiving, and there to bid us "goodbye." . . . So with the whole of mental experience, the energy-scheme leaves it aside and does not touch it. Our mental experience is not open to observation through any sense-organ. All that the scheme submits *is* thus open. The perceptible and the energy-scheme are co-extensive, for both are for us rooted in sense. Our mental experience has no such channel of entrance to the mind. It is already of the mind, mental.[1]

Sherrington makes two assertions here of interest: (a) experiences of seeing, hearing, etc., are not describable in the language of physics and physiology, i.e., of biophysics, and (b) our experiences of seeing, hearing, etc., are not publicly perceptible. The tone of these and other assertions made by Sherrington indicates that he also believes (c), namely, that (a) and (b) are conceptually *odd* or *strange*.

In asserting (a) Sherrington is in effect denying, as we did in the preceding chapter, the identity hypothesis. He emphasizes that we describe the operations of our brains in one kind of language and our experiences in another. One language includes alpha rhythms, millivolts, electrical impulses and so on, whereas the other mentions colors, sounds, tastes, etc. Sherrington details the differences between the two languages to emphasize that brain states are one sort of phenomena and conscious experiences quite another. His point in (a) is the *prima facie* case against the identity theory (that our experiences are really identical with states of our brains). For reasons given in the preceding chapter, we think this *prima facie* evidence stands; brain-states are defined in terms of properties very different from those attributable to our experiences. But, to repeat the point of the preceding chapter, this no more suggests a philosophical distinction between the mental and physical than refusing to identify books and tables implies a philosophical distinction between bookness and tableness. There is no more requirement to show why an experience *cannot be* a brain-state than there is to show why a book cannot be a table.

We must agree also with (b). Our experiences of seeing, hearing, etc., are not publicly perceptible. I cannot see your seeing and you cannot hear my hearing. But this is because experiences are not perceptible at all. I cannot perceive my experience of seeing the mouse, and you cannot perceive your experience of hearing the mouse. We *have* our experiences, or we are *aware* of our experiences, but we cannot perceive them through any sense organ. But, as argued in the preceding chapter, this fact cannot support a philosophical mental-physical distinction. Because *co*-awareness of our experiences seems *possible*, and because some *bodily* sensations and other events are *in fact* only privately known, privacy of awareness is not a philosophical criterion of the mental.

What are we to say about (c)? How does one decide whether it is *odd* or strange that our experiences are not publicly perceptible and that they are not describable in the language of nerve impulses and synapses? If one *expected* all occurrences to be describable in the vocabulary of biophysics, then our experiences would seem odd. But do persuasive reasons exist for encouraging such an expectation?[2] One would think, to the contrary, that routine experience discourages it. Furthermore, from the perspective of biophysics, experiences in themselves are not mysteries. Consider the detailed information, compared to what was available in Plato's time, that we now possess about the dependence of experiences of seeing, hearing, etc., upon specific regions of the brain. Experiences, after all, are states of the organisms that we are, and we know enough about them that it seems odd to say that, from a biophysical perspective, experiences are themselves oddities. Specific types of experiences may be queer; no good explanation may yet exist, for example, of the *déjà vu* kind of experience. Experiences peculiar to schizophrenics may not yet be understood, but it is surely odd to think that all experience is a scientific enigma. Human experience does not fall outside biophysics, so far as *explanation* is concerned. It does fall outside it, insofar as experiences are not describable in the language of this new science. But, again, why should anyone think that an oddity?[3]

2. Perceiving as Experiencing

Our experiences can strike us as slippery things. They may seem to disappear just when we expect to find them. You might think this particularly true of perceptual experiences. For instance, you now see this book, and to see a book is to have an experience. You have no difficulty in describing the book that you see, but what happens when you are asked to describe your *experience of seeing* the book? You probably get a frustrating sense of failure. For, as hard as you try, you always end up describing the book but not your seeing it. You simply draw a blank when, as it were, you try to detach your seeing the book from the book in order to give it a separate description. You certainly see the book, and that is certainly an experience, but when you turn to describe the experience, it vanishes.

One solution for the case of the disappearing experience is startling, for it says that perceiving is not experiencing. You cannot find the experience of seeing the book, because there is no such experience. Gilbert Ryle, following Aristotle, has written that "The verb 'to see' does not signify an experience, i.e. something that I go through, am engaged in."[4] He reaches this conclusion by noting how we can and cannot use the word "see." For instance, you can ask me whether I am looking for, looking at, staring at, or gazing at the book. And you can ask me how long I was engaged in looking for, looking at, staring at, or gazing at the book. Looking for the book is of course different from seeing it, but so also are looking, staring, gazing at. You can look, stare, gaze at a book without seeing it. Notice next how queer it sounds to ask me if I am *now seeing* the book or to ask me how long I *was seeing* it. Notice how peculiar is the question, "Were you seeing the chair when he jumped on it?" Experiences are processes or states, and you can always be asked whether you are undergoing them now and how long they endured. But this is precisely what Ryle holds you cannot bend the word "see" to mean. The obvious queerness of questions like "Are you seeing the car now?" and "How long were you seeing the car?" shows that the word "see" is being misused. He interprets this fact as meaning that "see" does not designate a process or state at all.

What it designates, Ryle explains, is an *achievement* rather than an experience or process spread out in time. Compare "see" with "win." So long as a person runs a race he is engaged in an activity, but as soon as he wins the race, his activity is terminated. His achievement, winning the race, is not itself an activity or process but rather the end or culmination of one. If verbs designate processes or activities of temporal duration, they are commonly used in the present tense. But present-tense uses of "see" and "win" tend to be awkward. We ask "Who *won* the race?" and, when he crosses the finish line first, we say, "He's *won* it." We ask "Who *saw* the thief?" and, when he detects the thief, we say, "He's *seen* him." In both cases, goes the explanation, something has been achieved, and what is reported is the termination of some process and not the commencement of one. So seeing is no more a process or experience than winning is a process or activity. Sherrington could not find a place for perceiving in his energy-scheme because there is actually no such process to be located anywhere.

B. A. Farrell also draws this conclusion.[5] His solution for the case of the disappearing experience is to abandon talking about "experience" altogether. The word is a philosophical trap. His recommendation is "Get rid of the nuisance words like 'sensation,' 'experience,' and so on, by defining them provisionally by means of concepts like: stimulus patterns, a discrimination by an organism, a readiness to discriminate, a discrimination of a discrimination." Try again to describe, not the book, but your experience of seeing it. Any description that occurs to you, Farrell insists, applies either to the book or to your response to the book. But do not confuse "response" with "experience." Philosophers and psychologists have traditionally meant by "experience" something different from behavior. This is a mistake, however, since there is no process, while you see the book, which can be called an "experiencing," in the sense that it is an occurrence in you that is quite different from how you behave. For instance, suppose you note that the book is blue. Noting that the book is blue *is behavior,* Farrell apparently wants to say. It is to make a response, to make a discrimination. When you describe what you note, that the book is blue, you describe a response or bit of behavior on your part. But you do not describe an "experience" of seeing a blue book, if you mean by "experience" an occurrence quite different from how you behave. Perceiving is discriminating, and discriminating is *doing.* There is no perceiving that is an experiencing by virtue of not being a doing. That is why you must always draw a blank when you try to describe your experience of seeing the book as a separate item, considered distinct both from the book and your discriminatory, behavioral responses to the book. No such separate item, to be called an "experiencing," exists.

What are we to think about these arguments? Ryle perhaps makes too much of the fact that the verb "to see" is subject to certain idiomatic restrictions. Suppose I continue to believe that "see" does signify a process or experience of temporal duration. I may be momentarily discomfited by the fact that "How long were you seeing the comet?" is ungrammatical, but I am quickly reassured by the fact that my query is expressible by "Over what period of time did you see the comet?" or by "How long was the comet seen by you?" and so on. The idiomatic roadblocks in the way of regarding seeing as experiencing seem easily surmountable. Further, Ryle appears to suggest that being a process and being an achievement are mutually exclusive. Truly, winning is not a process like running. But playing the harp or holding a weight are processes or activities that are also achievements. Once the objections based on idiomatic variations are removed, I can continue to view perceiving as more akin to playing a harp than to winning a race. Perceiving is simultaneously an achieving and an experiencing.

But my seeing the book, compared with my playing the harp, is so *motionless* that I have been accustomed to calling it an "experience" rather than an activity. I can just sit quietly and have experiences, whereas engaging in an activity requires that I bestir myself. Farrell perhaps strains the concepts of doing and behaving in insisting that what we normally call our "experiences" are really *behavioral* responses. If what we usually call "experiences" are reclassified as behavioral responses or as something else, then we will of course be unable to describe the anticipated "experience" of seeing the book; it will have vanished through being reclassified. But perhaps Farrell is involved in reclassifying too ruthlessly here. Suppose we concede that there may be an element of doing, activity, or behavior in any experience, that the contrast between behaving and experiencing is not precise. Reading a book is more active than merely seeing it, but both are less behavioristic than running or jumping. Ordinarily, we contrast having an experience with overt behavior, as when we speak of the experiences that *accompany* overt actions like running and jumping. This contrast is rooted in experience, and, even if not absolutely sharp, it needs to be preserved for what it is. It is genuinely confusing, however, to be told that what we normally call "experiencings," including occurrences as "motionless" as perceivings, are really *behavioral* responses, and that, therefore, there

But it may also be that Ryle and Farrell do not sufficiently appreciate how the case of the disappearing experience actually arouses your detective instincts. Their arguments may seem peripheral to the mystery. Suppose you are enjoying the sight of your new puppy. When you describe what it looks like, are you describing your experience of seeing the puppy as well as the puppy, or are you describing *only* the puppy? The experience of seeing the puppy vanishes when you seem forced into saying that you are describing *only* the puppy. For if reporting what a thing looks like is not to report a visual experience, then surely no kind of report can be conceived as being a report of visual experience.

A. M. Quinton makes your experience disappear, because, if he is right, you *are* forced into concluding that your description of what the puppy looks like is a description of the puppy only. He writes that we describe experience "very much less often than is usually supposed" and that "the description of experience proper is a sophisticated procedure and one seldom called for. It is an essential accomplishment for painters, broadcasting engineers, doctors of the eye and ear, cooks and experimental psychologists."[6] When you look about you and describe what you see, Quinton thinks that you are describing the things seen but *not anything else* to be called your "experience of seeing" them. Only rarely do you describe your experience, on those uncommon occasions when you are led to introspect your response to a painting, to a lover, to a tragic event, and so on. But the ordinary seeing of things is much too routine and pedestrian to invite introspective scrutiny, and thus describing what one sees is hardly ever the description of one's experience. So Quinton really makes the experience disappear in a manner not quite matched by Ryle and Farrell. He has you describing the puppy and only the puppy, not even a behavioral response in addition.

We should not forget how startling a conclusion this is. For we naturally assume, all of us, that when we see our puppies we are having visual experiences, and that when we tell what our puppies look like, we are *also* conveying what our visual experiences of them are like. We naturally assume that when we describe *what* we see, hear, touch, taste, or smell we are also describing an *experience* of seeing, hearing, touching, etc. We think that we almost always, whereas Quinton thinks that we virtually never, describe our experiences in describing what we perceive. We find some experiences very difficult to articulate, but it never seems to us that all experience is like that or that the only times we express our experiences are when we frown-ingly introspect. Certainly, painters may note details in the sunset overlooked by us, broadcasting engineers may catch nuances in the symphony ignored by us, and cooks may detect blemishes in the taste of the sauce unnoticed by us. But this surely only shows that they describe their perceptual experiences in greater detail than we do, not that we fail to describe such experiences completely. We have no good reason to surrender our normal assumption that descriptions of how things look and sound are *also* descriptions of perceptual experiences. The disappearing experience is restored to view. Indeed, *perceptual experience* may seem elusive to some philosophers just because, in its grosser detail anyway, it is so easy to describe. One learns how to do it without introspective hesitations.

But, it may be asked, can I actually distinguish, while I enjoy the rainbow, between how the rainbow looks and my experience of seeing it? Ought I not to have that ability, since I have just insisted, as a piece of justifiable common sense, that describing how the rainbow looks is also describing my visual experience of it? I say that I am describing two things at once, but can I really separate out those two things within my conscious experience? And if I cannot separately identify the look of the rainbow from my visual experience of it, then Quinton is perhaps right in believing that only one thing, the rainbow, is being described?

The fact is that I cannot distinguish between how a thing looks and my visual experience while I look at it. So far as my awareness is concerned, they are one and the same. I can make no sense of the request to describe one rather than the other, and we could leave it at that if our perceptual experience were infallible. However, subsequent experiences sometimes reveal an error in my description of how a thing now looks or sounds, and the discrepancy between my experience and how the thing really appears becomes evident. I am chagrined if my new tapestry does not really look like what I thought it looked like in the shop, but I am buoyant in finding that my new chandelier does look like what I said it did in the showroom. When correct, I describe both my visual experience and how the thing looks; when incorrect, in respect of the error, I describe only my visual experience. But the distinction is not revealed within one perceptual experience but is only revealed by one such experience checking another. Though the distinction is not introspectible, it is discoverable. In each case, its discovery is also a recovery of the *experience of perceiving* that, for reasons now sufficiently examined, might be thought to have disappeared.

3. Particular Experiences

Our experiences can strike us as slippery things, insofar as the concept of a *particular* experience can seem slippery. But, first, a note about where the problem does not exist. We all know how to identify particular, specific objects, like the clock on my desk, or particular occurrences, like the moving reflection of the taxi in my window. We also speak of particular experiences, like the embarrassing interview I had yesterday, the exciting movie seen recently, the boat ride this morning, and so on. We talk of particular experiences when we tell how we spent an afternoon or evening, and this presents no problem. We also talk of particular, momentary experiences, specifying them in terms of what we heard or saw or what we seemed to hear or see. Hopefully, any problems presented by this were solved in the preceding section.

To the extent that perceptual experiences are specified through the things perceived, experiences are like objects. To this extent, experiences are neither more nor less slippery than the objects we perceive. But there is an important respect in which our perceptual experiences are quite unlike perceptual objects. They are, in certain details, more akin to "fields of vision" than to specific objects found in such fields. It is certainly sensible to speak of "particular" fields of vision, since I have no difficulty in contrasting the particular "field" present when I stare at the street from the particular "field" present when I stare at the river. A particular field of vision consists of the things appearing in it.

A field of vision, however, is spatially unlike physical objects in being indeterminate at its limits. My field of vision has no recognizable shape or outline, as does my Queen Anne table. In switching attention from the street to the river, I change my fields of vision, but I am not aware of one field being circular and the other rectangular. My field of vision is the limit of what I see, but it bounds what I see without presenting a boundary describable spatially. You cannot in fact inspect the boundary of your field of vision as you can the boundaries of specific things appearing in it. If you shift attention to the extreme left, right, above, or below of your present visual field, you really change it for another, since in the process you both omit former ingredients and include new ones. No matter, then, how detailed you make your description of your visual experience of the river, it will be necessarily incomplete because it becomes vague and hesitant at the boundaries. Compared to the particularity of visual objects, the specificity of visual experiences thus seems elusive. We seem incapable of achieving a *complete* awareness of our visual experiences, their boundaries being the inexpressible limits of what we can say.

Moreover, we may be led to compare *all* visual experience with the appearance of an object, whose boundaries, because of the poor light or for other reasons, can only be apprehended indistinctly. The object may seem to expand and contract, disintegrate and reunify, temporarily losing its identity in merging with its surroundings. Perhaps visual experiences, whose spatial boundaries must be indistinct, really do merge with their surroundings? And these surroundings might be "larger" experiences? Perhaps a "particular" experience is part of a larger one, as a waterdrop can be included in a larger one? Our thinking in this direction may accelerate if we add that the *temporal* boundaries of experiences can also be vague. The particularity of an experience whose temporal boundaries elude fixing can seem a slippery thing. In some cases we may only be able to specify when one visual experience has been succeeded by another by reference to one act or span of attention being succeeded by another. A long eyeblink may mark such a succession, but in many instances we simply do not know, because the concept of one act of attention succeeding another is vague. This insures that some experiences will seem indeterminate at their temporal as well as spatial edges, and we may therefore be even more tempted to think of such experiences as mingling, blending, coalescing with others, analogous to the way an object, whose boundaries are indistinct to us, seems to blend into its surroundings.[7]

But this way of thinking, unfortunately, is generated by a confusion in our discussion of the boundaries of an experience. A note on what was said about *spatial* boundaries will suffice. What was truly said is that fields of vision and visual experiences are limited spatially, and it is difficult if not impossible to inspect the things near the limits without altering the range of attention, i.e. the field of vision. But what we said carried also the misleading suggestion that the spatial boundaries of visual fields and experiences are *unexaminable parts* of those fields and experiences. The fact, of course, is that they are not parts of anything whatever, for they are not things of any sort. You indicate the limit of your visual experience when you indicate the final thing you can see in any direction. However, you may come to think of the limit as itself a thing defying description, if you think of it as analogous to the boundary, say, of a table. But *that* is an observable surface, having spatial dimensions, etc., whereas the boundary of my visual experience is not a surface, neither thick nor thin. Once the confusing nature of the analogy of "experiences with limits" with "objects with boundaries" is realized, then so disappears the temptation to conceive of experiences as mingling with "larger" ones, as indistinctly apprehended objects can seem to merge into their surroundings in a "watery" way.

But there remains a respect in which particular experiences can be genuinely slippery. It may be that I am unable to notice consciously everything that I am presently seeing, hearing, smelling, feeling, etc. Perhaps my current experience includes, beyond what I can consciously notice, things of which I am *unconsciously aware*. Since the particularity of my present experience is just the totality of all the particular things seen, heard, etc., it may be too rich for my conscious apprehension.

Does a particular experience ever include unconscious awareness or the subliminal perception of things? Professional psychology appears divided in its answer here.[8] But does it not seem plausible that we see and hear on occasion more than we consciously notice? Our attention may be so distracted that it cannot, at the time, make a note of the fact that some detail is being seen, heard, tasted, etc. Is this not *prima facie* plausible? Moreover, we sometimes seem to remember what we did not consciously focus on at the time, like remembering that the clock struck four times though not remembering that one heard the strokes as they occurred. Furthermore, sometimes we apparently behave as if we saw something, when, for example, we repeatedly purchase a certain brand of cigars after being subliminally exposed to the brand name in a television advertisement, even though we neither consciously noticed it nor later remember having seen it. That we did see the brand name, though unconsciously, *may* be the simplest explanation of our new predilection for these cigars.

When we consider how much there is to see, hear, smell, taste, and touch, on some occasions, it seems reasonable to suppose that we "experience," i.e., unconsciously apprehend, more than we can consciously put into focus. When we also consider that subsequent behavior, independent of memory, can by itself serve as evidence for the hypothesis that one unconsciously perceived a thing, we can appreciate how exhaustive the tests must sometimes be to *disprove* the hypothesis. My inability to recall having seen an old friend in the opposite window is normally sufficient evidence that I did not see him. But if I later have certain dreams involving him, talk more often about him, become curious about the opposite window, and then independent evidence shows that he had appeared when I would probably have seen him, my inability to recall may be discounted in concluding that I did really but unconsciously see him.

An interesting explanation has recently been offered for the fact, previously known, that we see very little while our eyes are moving. Experiments apparently show that our seeing capacity is reduced to virtually zero during active eye movements. More remarkably, our seeing is reduced almost 50 per cent approximately 20 milliseconds (20-thousandths of a second) *before* we move our eyes and almost 50 per cent approximately 35 milliseconds *after* we cease moving our eyes. Since the eye movements themselves cannot cause the before-and-after blockage, the hypothesis is now suggested that the visual center of the brain contributes to the reduction of sight in such cases.[9] Extensive testing yields such results as a statistical fact. In individual cases, however, even more testing may be needed to insure the truth of the experimenters' reports. For, again, determining what was seen, as well as how much of it, depends not merely upon a person's testimony in immediate recall but also upon his subsequent behavior. Individual instances can represent interesting exceptions to the statistical rule. So we should not be astonished if someone now and then indicates that he saw, though unconsciously, a good deal even with his eyes moving.

The slipperiness of some particular experiences must be conceded. We can take in only so much at a time, and if we focus here then we neglect there. So the picture of our inner lives as a kind of foliated jungle hard to decipher is often a correct one. Some people, sensitive and introspectively adept, can penetrate that jungle better than others. Our experiences are of course sometimes plain and simple, and no suspicion need be aroused that more is happening to us than we consciously note. But we also often rightly infer that much of importance, beyond what shows to consciousness, is being experienced. Knowing oneself in knowing what one is experiencing can demand considerable agility of attention.

4
Thought

1. Thinking

Descartes' concept of mind led him to assert that humans *always* think—an odd claim indeed. But suppose we ask, when are we *not* thinking? Even when asleep or drugged we sometimes think, as our memories inform us. One may awake exhausted from trying to solve a problem during a fretful night. It is hard not to think. While watching a game, I may think about an incident of yesterday; while cycling, I may also be composing a sonnet; while responding to your orders, I may be imagining myself giving them. Even as I try not to remember a hateful conversation, scraps of it ambush my attention.

Suppose I'm experiencing an intense pain, and nothing else enters consciousness. Assume that I am not thinking about the pain, wondering what causes it, how it can be checked, or why I should be so victimized. It is simply that my whole attention is riveted on the pain. On such an occasion, am I thinking or not? Ordinary uses of "think" will actually permit you to argue either way. We use the word to cover everything from pondering a problem in logic to concentrating on a headache, and it is this fact that can make us wonder whether we always think or not. Since "think" is applied to any mental activity whatever, the consequence is, unless we impose semantic refinements, that we do think most of the time. This is evidently all that Descartes meant, so his assertion that we always think is not the oddity it initially seemed.

Psychologists explore specialized concepts of thinking. They tell us about the distinguishing features of directed thinking, productive thinking, imaginative thinking, thinking by association, extrapolation, interpolation, insight, and so on.[1] They generally shun trying to formulate something common to all varieties of thinking. However, A. J. Ayer, it appears, believes that *all* thinking is united by involving the use of symbols. Thinking *is* the intelligent use of symbols. Ayer emphasizes this while denying that "acts" of thinking occur. His claim is that thinking is not a "mental act" or experience but rather a disposition to use symbols intelligently.[2] Thinking is not an experience but an ability or skill that we can exercise without necessitating our having distinctive or special experiences. Ayer is correct to this extent: Asked to add some figures, I do so, name a sum, and honestly report no awareness of any special "thinking" experience; yet I did add the figures, and, precise or not, my performance is considered thoughtful, an instance of a person thinking. This makes thinking look like knowing how to operate with symbols, but not like headaches or images or other things that we "experience."

But, of course, we *do* speak of thinking as something that we experience. We say that we experience ourselves thinking when, for example, we are aware of our imaginings, ponderings, plannings, reveries, etc. We call it thinking when words and phrases slip in surprising succession through consciousness. This leads us to think of thinking as an experience that *happerns* to us rather than as something that we *do*. Why does Ayer ignore these considerations and focus instead upon what we take to be a restricted, specialized concept of thinking? The ability to use symbols intelligently is surely not the sole basis for declaring a person to be thoughtful or thinking. Ayer perhaps fails to distinguish between the process of thinking and the proof that the process occurred. The proof that I added the figures *think-*

ingly is in my use of symbols, the mathematical ones on paper and the verbal ones in testimony about what I did and why I did it. But sometimes the process of thinking itself might more accurately be described as awareness of symbols autonomously *entering* my consciousness rather than my *using* them consciously. Proving to you that I did have such an experience of thinking does, of course, require the deliberate use of symbols. Assuming, as Ayer does, that thinking is always a skillful doing, and remembering that the proof is in the pudding, maybe he does conclude that the thinking is in its proving. But this is a mistake, indeed a prevalent one as we want next to show. Consequently, we shall not labor the point that thinking is often an experience and not merely an ability to use symbols intelligently.

2. Naked Thought

Thinking, according to most theorists, is always clothed. It never occurs naked but is garmented in images, words, or symbols of some kind. But can we ever glimpse the thinking apart from the garments? Some say that is hopeless. Ayer dismisses the question as illegitimate, since thinking is said by him to *be* the *use* of symbols, not something "behind" or "clothed in" the symbols. He warns us, in effect, against the garment metaphor; thinking of thinking as naked or clothed only generates confusion.

Some psychologists, however, have believed that though thought usually occurs clothed in symbols, it *can* occur naked. They go further than Aristotle, who held that, while thought and imagery are not identical, thought cannot occur without imagery. Proponents of "imageless thought," of thought that *can* occur apart from words and from sensory things like images, were the Würzburg psychologists.[3] Their experiments in the first decade of this century led to much debate in the 1920's and 1930's about imageless thought. Imposing figures in psychology severely criticized the Würzburg group. Wilhelm Wundt, for example, argued that their experiments did not meet scientific standards, and E. B. Titchener attributed their claims of finding imageless thoughts to faulty introspecting. Titchener's conviction was that all thinking is constituted of sensory items like images, sensations, or feelings. He believed that his hypothesis is verifiable introspectively. A loud controversy erupted, therefore, when the psychologists at Würzburg contended that their introspections disproved Titchener's hypothesis. The difficulty of resolving the dispute contributed to the decline of introspection as an investigatory technique and to the ascendance of behaviorism. Psychologists began to concentrate upon the public behavior rather than the private introspections of the human organism; animal and human psychology no longer looked so different.

The Würzburgers wanted to learn what is distinctively happening when a person is thinking. In one type of experiment the subject was asked a question; the time of his response of a mandatory "yes" or "no" was checked by a stopwatch, after which he reported as carefully as possible what had occurred in his consciousness as he deliberated his answer. Two distinguished psychologists, Dürr and Külpe, served as subjects. Dürr was asked whether the future is just as much a condition of the present as of the past. He answered "no" ten seconds later. He then reported: "First I thought: That sounds like something correct (without words). Then I made the attempt to represent it to myself. The thought came to me: Men are determined by thoughts of the future. Then, however, immediately the thought: *that the thought of the future should not be confounded with the future itself; that such confusions, however, constitute a frequent dodge in philosophical thought. (Of words or images there was throughout no trace.) Thereupon the answer: No.*" [4]

Külpe was asked whether, when he thought of purpose, he had also to think of chance and folly. He answered "yes" 11.5 seconds later. His report of his deliberating was this: "It was difficult and strange (*ungeläufig*) for me to bring purpose into contrast with the two others. That is to say, the thought darkly emerged that the two others must be presupposed by purpose, in the same way as not–A is by A. Folly I succeeded, without more ado, in bringing into this scheme; with chance I did not succeed. Then I had the thought, *how, with Darwin, chance is considered as an explanation of purpose. (There were no images, not a trace of the word Darwin, this is the first time I have spoken the word. It was an immediate, quite clear knowledge* (knowing)."[5]

Other experiments were used with similar results. Given a certain stimulus, and then asked to study carefully what the stimulus prompted in the way of thoughts, the Würzburgers agreed that it was often a case of *naked* thoughts being present to their awareness. George Humphrey writes that they found a thinking process that "shows no sensory quality, no sensory intensity. Something of which we may rightly predicate degree-of-clearness, degree of certainty, a vividness by means of which it arouses our psychic interest; which, however, in its content is quite differently determined from everything that is ultimately reducible to sensations; something for which it would be nonsense to try to determine whether it possessed a greater or less intensity, or even into what sensory qualities it could be resolved."[6] Humphrey concludes that, on the issue of imageless, nonsensory, nonverbal, or naked thought, the Würzburgers were more accurate than their critics.[7]

It is an important fact that some psychologists believe the hypothesis of naked thought to have been verified experimentally. This tends to be unappreciated in current philosophical psychology or "philosophy of mind," but it seems to us that ordinary experience testifies to what the Würzburg experiments are believed to prove. Two kinds of common experiences are easily cited. Most of us know what it is to have a particular thought while vainly groping for the words to express it. We know the thought, but the words for it elude us; when the proper words come to mind, we recognize that they do formulate what we were thinking. Secondly, our thoughts often occur so rapidly that we have no time in which to formulate them verbally. But sometimes we manage to hold them in memory, and retrospectively we take the required time for verbalizing them. These experiences certainly show that we can have naked thoughts, thoughts that are neither identical with nor expressed in words, images, feelings, or emotions. There is no mystery about them, we know what they are like. They can be short-lived or endure a while, can obsess us, can tantalize our memories, and so on. As images, sensations, and feelings are states of the organisms that we are, so are naked thoughts. They are states of ourselves that we learn to recognize, as just said, through ordinary experience. In all probability, it was such experience that led the Würzburg psychologists to try to describe what happens when a person is thinking. In any event, it is such ordinary experience that can help us to appreciate how the Würzburg experiments verified, not merely the hypothesis of imageless or naked thought, but, more significantly, the variety of occasions when it occurs.

Yet we owe an explanation. If naked thoughts stare us in the face, so to speak, why are contemporary philosophers blind to them? Why the current propensity to assert that thinking is either the use of words or requires expression in them? One reason is that some thinkers do not trust ordinary experience, presuming that the issue of naked thought is to be decided experimentally. Perhaps Titchener will be vindicated, and thoughts will be at least analyzable into the images of words even if not into words themselves. But, with the exception of a few like Humphrey, psychologists have ignored our topic, and it seems that the Titchenerian project of introspectively dissecting conscious experiences into sensory ingredients is nowhere in prospect of being revived. Philosophers are thus thrown back upon their own resources here, and ordinary experience, as often happens, may be reconsulted as counsel for the decision.

Another reason is that today's philosophy is preoccupied with language, and consequently thought is important insofar as it is examinable in language. Naked thought, even if real, is uninteresting. What is important about thinking is its structure or logic, says today's fashion, and that is found in its linguistic formulation. A thought has not really been *produced* until it has been put adequately into words. You can only study a thought for its structure and logic insofar as it is a linguistic thing. You have not even *communicated to yourself* what is your thought until you have "languaged" it. But this line of thinking and its preoccupation with language is confusing. *Producing* and *communicating* (even if only to oneself) thoughts do require verbalization, whereas simple *knowledge* of one's thoughts does not. To suppose it does is to commit the error, noted in the preceding section, of confusing the process of thinking with a proof of its occurrence. Because the latter necessitates linguistic symbolizing, it does not follow that the former does, and our claim is that ordinary experience shows that it sometimes does not.

But is the issue important? Yes, for this reason: If we do not trust our awareness of preverbal thoughts, only accept as actual states of ourselves what we methodically put into words, we are alert to but a fraction of ourselves. Self-knowledge is conspicuously incomplete. Possibly the goal of total self-acquaintance is as undesirable as it is unrealizable. However, if the search for knowledge of self must respect limits, accept blinders, these surely refer not to quantity but to specificity of information. We suffer not from how much but from *what* we know about ourselves. Daily rather than laboratory experimenting can reveal what we ought and ought not to know about ourselves. We see the issue of naked thought as part of the practical problem of asking what more about oneself, including nonverbalized thoughts, one ought to know in behalf of a richer psychological life. Logically and grammatically, the linguistic garment of the thought is what counts. Psychologically, that it occurs, clothed or not, is what matters.

3. Inner Speech

Psychologists are interested in the phenomenon of inner speech, that subtle process whereby we think or speak silent words to ourselves. Most thinking occurs as inner speech, in unsounded words or fragments of words. The tendency of philosophers to identify thinking with the production of words leaves inner speech unappreciated. Considered merely as overt speech minus sound, its distinctive features go unnoticed.[8] An important type of thinking is thus misunderstood, and the habit of regarding the verbalization of thoughts but not the thoughts themselves is reinforced. Without the hypothesis of naked thought, we shall argue, it is difficult to explain the peculiarity of inner-speech thinking.

Lev S. Vygotsky has written illuminatingly about inner speech.[9] He takes issue with a theory once suggested by Jean Piaget. According to Vygotsky, the cornerstone of Piaget's theory of child development is his account of egocentric thinking in the child. The infant's thought is initially *autistic,* essentially unconscious of its goals and needs, concerned with the gratification of wishes in a fantasy of imagination and dreams. The infant lives in his own world because yet unaware of the real environment. The next step in the child's growth is *egocentric* thinking. Piaget observes that the youngster's speech is now mainly about and to himself. His egocentric speech is a babbling accompaniment to whatever he is doing. There is no genuine interest in communication. Egocentric speech, Piaget's studies show, dominates the preschool child's talk, and about 45 per cent of the talk of seven-year-olds is reported to be egocentric. As *socialization* increases, egocentric thinking decreases. It does not immediately disappear but gradually evaporates, since it has no function in the youngster's maturing relation to his environment. His thinking and speech become increasingly social and concerned with the real world rather than imaginative gratifications. Egocentric thinking, therefore, represents for Piaget (in his earlier studies) a transient phase in the child's development. It is more akin to autistic thinking, tapering off when socialized thinking takes over.

Vygotsky, on the other hand, says that his experiments reveal that the child's thinking does *not* move from autistic to egocentric to social. Morover, he argues that Piaget has misunderstood the character of egocentric thought and has, consequently, failed to offer an adequate theory of inner-speech thinking.[10] Vygotsky reverses Piaget's order of maturation. His experiments, he claims, show the earliest speech and thinking of the child to be *social,* consistent with the fact that all speech is mainly communicative. Young and old alike use words for reaching others. According to Vygotsky, egocentric speech develops when the child "internalizes" outward behavior. An example of this is a child's duplicating in a dialogue with himself an argument he has witnessed between two other youngsters. Egocentric speech, talking to oneself, has the special function, Vygotsky believes, of growing into inner speech, and inner speech is distinctive in expressing both autistic and social (also logical) thinking. Vygotsky contrasts his theory of development—initially social, then egocentric, then inner speech—with Piaget's as just described above, and also with the behaviorist's theory of first vocal speech, then whisper, and finally inner speech.

Vygotsky's experiments indicate the social origin of egocentric speech or thinking. Preschool children, who exhibited egocentric speech in the presence of other children, virtually abandoned it when placed in the company of deaf–mute children or children speaking a foreign language. A decrease in egocentric speech occurred when a child was put into a lonely situation or with strange children. When the child was told not to talk loudly but only in whispers, or was placed where a noisy orchestra played nearby, his egocentric talk fell off noticeably. These facts supported what Piaget, in fact, had already noticed— that egocentric talk occurs mainly in the presence of other egocentric-speaking children, that the child has the illusion that his talking to himself is really understood by his companions, and the egocentric speech is more like overt speech than it is like inaudible whispering. Vygotsky's point is that his theory that egocentric speech is a transition from social to individual thinking better squares with these facts than does Piaget's, which has it just in reverse.

Egocentric speech, Vygotsky claims, is not merely a babbling accompaniment to the child's activities. It is, though still basically social, a type of thinking that is on the way to more internal, personal thinking. It is moving toward transformation into inner speech, the phenomenon emphasized in Vygotsky's theory of language and thought. "Our experiments convinced us that inner speech must be regarded, not as speech minus sound, but as an entirely separate speech function. Its main distinguishing trait is its peculiar syntax. Compared with external speech, inner speech appears disconnected and incomplete." [11] Advanced egocentric speech and inner speech both display the feature of condensation. The tendency is to drop the subject of a sentence and associated words and to retain only the predicate. This happens because, in thinking or talking to oneself, one knows what the subject is. One needs fewer words. As Vygotsky says, "Inner speech is speech almost without words." [12]

Vygotsky rightly emphasizes how inner and overt speech differ. The latter is not the result of simply vocalizing the former, as some philosophers, hoping to assimilate all thinking into the production of words, seem to believe. A complex psychological process is required to transmute inner speech into overt communication. Vygotsky also properly emphasizes the distinction between even inner speech and what we have called "naked" thought. While we do not grasp all that he says about thought as distinguished from speech, we agree that the "flow of thought is not accompanied by a simultaneous unfolding of speech" and that "thought, unlike speech, does not consist of separate units." [13] It seems clear that, without the hypothesis of naked or nonverbal thought, the kind of thinking exemplified in inner speech is very hard to explain. How can we be aware of *complete* thoughts at times when only a single word, or a fragment of a word, is present to consciousness? The single word or fragmentary symbol seems to function like the stimulus in the Würzburg experiments. It prompts a naked thought, a nonsensory state of the organism, and in knowing it the organism that I am knows what it thinks then and there. With time, luck, and ability, I can give it a verbal formulation and publish it for you and even for myself.

What and when do I think? This question, we have argued, is not answerable adequately if I look only at my verbal productions. This is true whether such productions are inner or overt. Knowing what and when I think is an obvious part of knowing oneself, and the claim here is that, if one attends only to one's words, one's self-acquaintance is inevitably spotty. This is not to denigrate the role of language in thinking. As Ludwig Wittgenstein emphasized, knowing a language is a condition for having complex thoughts.[14] Without a language I could not think, for instance, that maybe an earthquake will occur three weeks from tomorrow, causing an angry telephone exchange between me and my insurance company. But, even if knowing a language is a condition for certain thoughts to originate, it does not follow that their every occurrence must be *in* words. Experience and not *a priori* theorizing must be the arbiter here. We must be alert, in our introspective experience, to our thoughts as well as to our words for knowing when and what we think and when it occurs in words and when it happens nakedly.

5

Motivation

1. Contemporary Research

We study psychology to learn *why* we do what we do. Theories of motivation are consulted for discovering what motivates us. Such theories cover what are now less fashionably known as instincts, impulses, needs, drives, etc. Psychologists assume that *something* illuminating can be said about the why of *anything* done by us as groups or individuals. It may be fragmentary and vague, but illuminating. Most of us probably share that conviction, one consequence being "parlor psychoanalysis." More than what we do, we may come to revere its "explanation." But our searching the why of our minutest doing is understandable. It is a special feature of our era, which historians may judge to be more a probing of ourselves than of outer space. Compared to what psychology, in its new affiliation with biochemistry and biophysics, is disclosing, knowing how to reach the moon is mere technology. Today's intellectual excitement, replacing what accompanied non-Euclidean geometries, relativity, and quantum theories, attends the recent psycho-bio-chemico-physical mixture of disciplines.

The actual or hypothetical information about ourselves is

formidable. Philosophical psychology must take an interest in the new information, realizing that its own emphases are partly responses to today's massive research on the human organism. The incredible daily flow of facts and hypotheses, all relevant to self-comprehension, necessarily influences the philosopher's conception of where his own contributions reside. A rapid sampling of what we are being told about ourselves makes the point.

For one thing, the family of man is given a longer history each time an anthropological study is released. One of the latest estimates, based upon paleontological findings in Kenya, is that our earliest ancestors were present 20 million years ago. Life itself is of course of much older origin. A rock formation discovered in South Africa, and known to be at least 3.1 billion years old, was found to contain 22 amino acids. These are the chemical building blocks of protein required by living organisms. Significantly, these have been recently laboratory-produced out of inorganic materials supposedly similar to primitive earth. Viruses, like living things in reproducing but unlike them in requiring a living cell to do it, have now been created in a test tube. The chemical evolution of life is increasingly confirmed.

We know more today about the dependence of our physiological reactions upon our hormones. These chemical substances can determine not only an organism's growth or sexual behavior but its capacity to learn. The chemistry of sleep progresses with the discovery that rats and cats fall asleep when given fluid from the spinal cords of sleepy goats. The chemical sleep-inducer, which is apparently interspecies transferable, is thought to be of small molecules carrying a weak electrical charge. Scientists have investigated whether memory and the effects of learning can be also transferred. The spectacular discovery of DNA (deoxyribonucleic acid), the controlling gene substance of the chromosomes, and of RNA (ribonucleic acid), manufacturing director of protein in living cells, is relevant here, in addition to its suggestion of how man can choose the character of future generations. Some scientists believe that

RNA is basic to the chemistry of memory, but experiments, designed to show whether memory is coded in RNA molecules and can be transferred from one organism to another, are presently inconclusive in their results. Still, the claim that future biochemistry will show how to transfer memory is a fascinating hypothesis.

We are even told that a man's ambition may be measured by the amount of uric acid in his blood. Uric acid is rather like caffeine in its chemical structure. Low levels of uric acid may be heightened by use of RNA, though studies here are in the early stages. Acetycholine, a chemical that is essential to the mechanics of our nervous systems, seems to have been found for the first time in brain tissue, but its relevance for nervous disorders remains to be seen. A virus is presently suspected as the cause of a strange brain disease, sometimes called Creutzfeld-Jakob disease, which has been injection-transmitted from a man to a chimpanzee. If discovered, the virus might be the key to unlock the mystery of other brain and nervous diseases. Brain research commands today's headlines. We read that a mother's diet while pregnant can profoundly affect her child's I.Q. (intelligence quotient). An inadequate supply of protein may result in a subnormal number of brain cells. Changes in diet, including addition of protein, are also reported to reduce complaints of persons suffering from indigestion, tension, and depression. We continue to learn that "we are what we eat."

Linus Pauling has recently stated that chemical imbalance in the brain may cause mental disorders. Deficiencies in vitamins and other chemical substances possibly affect the brain and nervous system, causing a "cerebral scurvy or cerebral pernicious anemia." Pauling's suggestion is that, because of the sensitive dependence of brain and nervous tissue upon their molecular composition, chemical treatment of mental aberrations will perhaps replace psychotherapy and electric shock treatments. In this connection, a chemical test originally developed at Harvard Medical School is said to be 90 per cent accurate in measuring the extent and severity of psychosis in

338 persons. The test detects a protein in the cerebrospinal fluid; the level of glyoprotein neuramic acid, a component of the brain's gray matter, is the yardstick used in the test. Insanity and stress, in other tests currently reported, apparently produce an imbalance in the hormones of the adrenal glands and in the body chemical, histamine.

How are we to prevent the mental retardation that afflicts 5 million Americans? Science assumes that it is due to a chemical deficiency, possibly of something like thyroxin, a thyroid hormone. Tests indicate that some mental diseases correlate with an oversecretion of the pituitary gland, and the possible link between criminal propensities and genetic abnormalities has been widely advertised. The vast studies of schizophrenia have not found the cure, but they indicate progress; perhaps a unique protein factor found in the blood of schizoids will be part of the answer.

The human brain weighs about three pounds. It is a mass of 10 billion nerve cells, receiving and transmitting messages from and to all parts of the body by means of electrochemical impulses traveling along the nerves at speeds of 2 to 200 miles an hour. Some thinkers predict that it is too complex to be understood as fully as we would like, but the research is immense. It was formerly thought that, deprived of his brain's left cerebral hemisphere, a man could not speak or write, sing, calculate, or discriminate colors, but this has recently been disproved. It now seems that a person can learn to use the other half of his brain to perform functions normally performed by the damaged half. A detailed mapping of brain areas and their functions is still in dispute, but specifics are known, including the fact that by destroying parts of the hypothalamic sections of rats' brains, hunger is induced in the rats. On the basis of such experiments, one theorist has postulated a model brain in which different components interact according to twelve rules or so. Dr. Delgado of Yale University, who stopped a bull's charge by sending radio signals to electrodes put in its brain, thinks radio stimulation of the brain may someday cure disease. His work shows that electrical stimulation of specific spots in

the brain evokes "frightened" or "friendly" reactions as anticipated.

There is now evidence that mental activity increases the size
of the brain. University of California investigators report that
the brains of rats and mice increased as much as 6 per cent
in size and weight after daily exposures to performance-
challenges, like learning to run a new pattern of barriers for
food. The parts of the brains regulating vision showed a weight
gain of 6 per cent, and, in various ways suggestive of further
research, the brains of rats stimulated by performance-
challenges showed an increased amount of enzymes. A much
publicized investigation is that at Western Reserve University.
Brains taken from monkeys are kept alive for testing. They are
"read" by the electroencephalograph, which measures brain
waves. The EEG tracings on the apparatus were sometimes
identical with those obtained from an alive and awake animal.
Some removed brains, retaining auditory nerves, responded to
cricket-type sounds. Just possibly, it is suggested, the detached
monkey brain is conscious, feels hunger and thirst.

Biological study of the brain has stimulated a "hardware"
imitation in the form of computers. So today we wonder how
the machines may beat us. The brain's electrochemical system
can be studied, simulated, perhaps improved upon. Electronic
simulation of the brain rouses strange-sounding hopes. Future
machines may display foresight. In some respects, electronic
brains already know how to teach themselves to learn, for
example, the difference between left and right, not unlike the
way a child does. Massachusetts Institute of Technology engineers have come up with a robot that builds towers out of toy
blocks. Its arms are metal claws, its eye a television camera, its
brain a computer, all collaborating to achieve a humanlike
robot performance. Computers win at chess, and no one really
knows the limits of their potential skills. Reputable scientists
have suggested that an electronic brain might burst the fourth
dimension. We cannot conjecture very well what that might
be until better brains find out and tell our present brains how
to grasp it. One step in that direction is assured, now that an

M.I.T. professor has a computer learning to understand English.

Our topic in this chapter is motivation. Current discussions of it will inevitably refer to the variety of "information" just sampled, all of it considered relevant when wondering what motivates the variety of human action. It is responsible for certain emphases in these chapters. Detailed comments on the details are pointless here, but to have a *sense* of the details of the scientific scene is important, as it sets guidelines for philosophical inquiry. Our response to today's information flow, taken by some as a challenge to our belief in human freedom, is represented later in the chapter, to which goal the next section points us.

2. Aggression

Theories about aggression, in animals and humans, are popular reading today.[1] We ponder the motivation of and the possible control of aggression. We fear it in ourselves, yet suspect we are born to it. We fasten, therefore, upon the current revival of the dispute whether aggression is an instinct or a learned response, whether it is an animal inheritance, whether it is good or bad, and so on.

Freud, in his later theory, postulated a type of aggressiveness, called the "death instinct," equal in rank with sexuality. His point was that we all instinctively seek our own destruction. Our aggression toward others is actually a temporary deflection of our more basic hostility toward ourselves. Freud's theory of aggression *toward others,* therefore, is kin to a contemporary influential theory developed by Yale University psychologists.[2] This theory denies that aggressiveness is instinctual, holding instead that it is always a result of some frustration. It has even been suggested that frustration always leads to aggression.[3]

But others see aggression as an instinct, existing prior to frustrations and not therefore their product. A British symposium on aggression prompted its convenors to write, "The current psychiatric evidence seems almost unequivocal; aggression is not merely a response to frustration, it is a deep-seated, universal drive."[4] This is the theme of Konrad Lorenz's popular *On Aggression*, supplemented by the argument that the aggressive instinct is originally constructive and is destructive only when its natural function is somehow perverted.[5]

Lorenz and other Continental ethologists, students of animal behavior "in the field," basing their concept of aggression as an innate animal inheritance upon the behavior of ducks, geese, coral fish, etc., are rebuked by other psychologists. One critic severely criticizes Lorenz, describing his book on aggression as unscientific and antirational.[6] He labels it a moral tract rather than reputable ethology. Lorenz is said to ignore recent research, not mentioning, for example, Harlow's work with rhesus monkeys that shows the social behavior of these monkeys to be learned and not, as once believed, instinctive. Another critic makes similar charges, noting that Lorenz omits any physiological description of aggression.[7] This is significant, since, according to the instinct hypothesis, aggression is "spontaneous" and does not require external stimulation. But the critic's point is that, though one part of the brain (the hypothalamus) is mechanically equipped to sustain and amplify external stimulation in the occurrence of *anger*, there is "no mechanism for building up the first stimulation from within. There is no internal change corresponding to the change in blood sugar which results in hunger."[8] But, if anger and aggression are instinctive in the sense of arising spontaneously from within the organism, then an internal mechanism corresponding to what happens with hunger is precisely what we ought to find. He then observes:

This may appear to be a fine technical point, but it has one important result. If Lorenz is right, then man cannot lead a happy, peaceful existence, but must continually be sublimating the spontaneous "drive" which accumulates within him. If the physiologists are correct, then it is theoretically possible for man to lead a happy and peaceful existence, provided he is not continually stimulated to violence. Sublimation will have its uses because in any practical situation there will always be some accidental stimulation toward violence, but it is only one of the many techniques provided by modern scientific knowledge for the control of aggression.[9]

This very sketchy recapitulation scarcely represents the amount of research and debate by psychology on the topic of aggression. Nor does it indicate the complexities involved, of how to define "instinct" and "aggression" itself. There is the problem of how to *measure* aggression, a problem aggravated by the fact that one kind of aggressive behavior arises from anger, while another is a habit and can occur without anger. Single-factor theories, like the frustration hypothesis, are vulnerable. "In the studies summarized, noxious stimuli have been the most effective instigators of aggression, whereas frustration (to which aggression would be a reaction) has not been very effective." [10] (Criticisms of the single-factor instinct hypothesis have already been noted.)[11]

Behavioral scientists will continue their search for the stimulants of aggressive responses. For example, Leonard Berkowitz offers evidence that violence in films arouses aggressive impulses in the watcher. A recent experiment shows that mice watching other mice in combat become aggressive. What is even more interesting is the discovery that a chemical change occurs in the brains of the aroused mice. The spectating mice exhibited a lowered level in the brain of norepinephrine, a chemical that transmits nerve messages in the brain.[12] It has also been discovered that injections of hormones (instead of electrical stimulation) into different parts of the brain elicit aggressive as well as other types of behavior.[13] The Experimentalists have an obvious advantage over the Instinctualists in recommending cures for violence. Lorenz urges sublimation of aggressiveness in more international sports and contests. But one critic notes that this is often proposed, but not in the name of ethology, and another calls it inferior to William James's proposal of a nonmilitary conscription program for youth in his famous "The Moral Equivalent of War" in 1910.[14] Also, it seems obviously naïve compared to the variety of cures recommended by the Experimentalists for the variety of aggressive responses they uncover.

So what do the Instinctualists hope to achieve by reviving the idea that aggression is an instinct? That virtually all of us are prone to violence in some circumstances is surely not at issue, for no one denies it. They appear, first, to want us to *accept* this, to admit rather than repress it. Too many of us feel guilty about the aggressiveness in ourselves, but this is unreasonable, inasmuch as our aggressiveness exists through instinct and not through choice. Feeling guilty about one's innate aggressiveness is a normal emotional (and intellectual) mistake. They seem, secondly, to want us to realize how erroneous is the identification of innate aggressiveness with proneness to violence. They rather think of natural aggressiveness as an energetic going-outwards, as opposed to a passive collapsing inside. Lorenz claims that such aggressiveness is good in animal life, that it is responsible for distributing animals into adequate territories for breeding and feeding, even for avoiding fights to the death.[15] Their basic point is perhaps this: Seeing aggression as instinctive will permit us to live in more cheerful acceptance of ourselves, which in turn will allow us to encourage the constructive, while discouraging the destructive, capacities of the instinct.

But the Experimentalist has an effective rejoinder. Who knows, he asks, what may be the disastrous consequences of people "accepting" their aggressions? Repression may be vastly superior to such acceptance. In any event, what people need to learn is not that aggressiveness is simply part of human nature but rather that it is modifiable. We *can* be its managers, not its lackeys. Secondly, the claim that aggression is not all bad and performs useful functions, even if true, is not an adequate safeguard. Accepting aggression as an instinct is like taking a wife: You must accept her entirely, and if she is as much saboteur as savior, you are menaced. *Evidence* instead of hunch is needed before concluding that the race will profit from becoming Instinctualists. The saddest moments in human history do seem the consequence of aggression being "accepted" in the extreme.

3. "Always a Cause"

In its search for the motivation behind the action, aggressive or otherwise, psychology creates new interest in an ancient philosophical controversy. Is everything, including human action, caused? If so, is man really free or not? Or are we only like automata, doing what previous events (the causes) necessitate? This metaphysical question comes to mind when one reads that "robots offer a way to simulate psychological processes. We reason that if we can understand a psychological process, we ought to be able to build a machine which puts that process into action. For example, if we propose a model for letter recognition, then we should be able to construct a robot that recognizes letters. If we are successful, then our model is at least an adequate solution. If our machine does not recognize letters, then clearly something is lacking in the theory."[16] When motivational theories are associated with this assertion, they may seem to undermine human dignity by picturing us as systems of passive responses to countless stimuli, as powerless to react other than we do.

The philosophical threat represented by motivational theories, however, does not press a focus on robots. Future robots may imitate humans remarkably, including the capacity to reproduce, and creatures much like ourselves may be created artificially. We shall then need to consider whether they, like us, are free or not. The suspicion that they and we are *not* stems from the philosophical principle that *all* action is motivated, that whatever the deed, there is *always a cause* behind it. We of course believe that some if not most of our actions are "free" *in the sense that we were not forced to do them and could have done something else instead.* But if we are led also to believe that all actions are motivated or caused, we may conclude that our actions are necessary effects of these causes, and that we could not have acted other than as we did and are hence not free. We seem, oddly, to want to believe two contradictory things.

Common sense will never abandon the conviction that our behavior is largely free, even if we occasionally and temporarily question it. And for excellent reasons! In particular cases it may be very difficult to determine whether a person's action was free or not. The evidence may be hard to locate. But we know, in general, what it is to secure evidence for concluding that someone was incapable of doing other than what he did. We know how to distinguish between free and helpless behavior, and common sense finds nothing in philosophy or psychology to obliterate the distinction. Common sense, accordingly, will work out of the two apparently conflicting beliefs by concentrating upon the philosophical principle. It will either declare the principle false, or it will find an interpretation of the principle that does not conflict with our belief in the general freedom of human action.

Common sense can remark that physiological psychology, for example, does not pretend to be in search of the motivators or causes of human action in general. It rather tells us what are the necessary conditions (brain and hormonal states, etc.) for normal behavior, what disturbances in those conditions produce abnormal action (schizoid, etc.), and how restoration to normality may be achieved. Physiological psychology is committed to the principle of "always a cause" when the organism behaves abnormally.[17] But, for its purposes, normal activity can be considered self-governing, without being attributed to some prior "cause," so long as the necessary conditions of brain and other physiological states occur. From this point of view, the principle of "always a cause," if taken unrestrictedly, is conceivably, in fact probably, false.

It can also be remarked that belief in "always a cause" leads philosophers into what we may call the "domino theory" of causality. This is the idea that causality is a relation between discriminable *events,* and that events related as cause and effect constitute "chains" indefinitely long backward and forward in time. If you, so to speak, knock one domino-event in a chain, you topple the whole chain. On this view, your doing something is a domino-event; if you undid it, you would topple an indefinitely long chain of events. But since this is hard to accept, it may seem easier to believe that you could not have behaved differently.

But, given the evidence, the domino theory appears fanciful. Suppose the question is why I choose a red rather than a green hat. Sometimes a prior cause-event, as required by the domino theory, can be located for the effect-event, my choosing the red hat. But more often it cannot. A motivational theory satisfies us, for instance, if it presents evidence that my choice of the hat is due to a *habit* (or disposition), which is not an event. Or we may accept an explanation of a statistical sort, attributing my choice to the fact (not event) that I belong to a class whose *tendency* is to prefer red hats. Or we may settle for a bedrock kind of explanation, which says that, except for unusual circumstances, it is just *my nature* (no event) to prefer red to green hats. Motivational theories in psychology are not usually constructed with an eye to supporting the domino theory of "always a cause." Some psychoanalytic theories are the exception, when they insist that, for certain neuroses, some traumatic childhood experience was "the" cause-event. Since such hypotheses are difficult if not impossible to test, they are not typical of experimental motivational psychology.

Theories of motivation, including those on aggression, are largely concerned with what happens to the organism because of the presence (or absence) of an *accumulation* of certain experiences. What motivates Johnny to react aggressively? Not this or that past event or experience, but rather an accumulation of such-and-such experiences. Psychology gets the assignment, not only of deciding which experiences are relevant, but also how to measure the effect of those experiences occurring together and successively. Is crawling more important for the child than lap-playing (and how much of it?) for motivating gentle rather than aggressive behavior ten years later? The answers provided by experiments are obviously tentative and imprecise; but they are partial answers yielding some illumination, though "how much" is most uncertain. Motivational psychology mainly works with the indefinite, hard-to-measure causal unit of "accumulated experience." It does not try to analyze this into more minute causal relations between this and that event (as the domino theory suggests). It rather attempts to approximate more closely how much of what blend of experiences will become a trait of the organism. There is "always a cause" means that there is always an opportunity for a more precise account of how an "accumulation" of experience affects subsequent developments in the human organism.[18]

4. Hidden Causes and Decision

Suppose, then, that we have expelled the worry that all behavior proceeds from brain or hormonal events. Suppose that we see comparisons of ourselves to the Uganda Kob and the hairy ape as fun rather than science; we therefore decline to attribute our aggressive or affectionate actions to an evolutionary deposit in our genes. Suppose we abandon trying to locate all motivation ultimately in tissue needs. Have we thereby guaranteed human freedom? The suspicion that hidden causes exist, even for actions that seem free, will survive unless exorcising remarks can be made about both behavioral "reinforcement" theory and general psychoanalytic theory. As much as they differ, both have contributed to the contemporary sense that there are always hidden causes; that, even when apparently in control, we are yet controlled. Both emphasize the controlling effects of accumulated experience.

B. F. Skinner is a major influence because of his success (requiring ingenious technical innovations) in teaching animals complicated behavior. He has already produced evidence that techniques used with rats and pigeons are applicable to human learning. Skinner has stressed "operant" behavior, what a pigeon, say, does *to* its environment, instead of the "respondent" behavior by the salivating dog to Pavlov's bell. In refusing "to go under the skin," he has rejected the imputed dependence of psychological investigation upon physiological hypotheses. His work shows that impressive results in animal training are achievable without reference to internal physiology. The desired responses in the animal evolve into a behavioral pattern by strategically exposing the animal to "reinforcing" stimuli, those increasing the occurrences of the wanted responses. Skinner may seem to have struck a blow for freedom in his ignoring of physiology and his concern for operant rather than respondent behavior. Yet, his technique of training is of course a form of conditioning, a mode of *control,* as he is frank to say. The organisms that we are thus appear controllable and predictable by the student of reinforcing stimuli.[19]

Freud's work, as everyone knows, is a testimonial to the (supposed) tyrannical effects of accumulating experiences in childhood. Freud concluded that behavioral patterns crystallize early and repeat themselves, become habits hard to break. He wrote in 1914 that what we repress and forget we nevertheless tend to repeat in action.[20] Our behavior, as repetition of past but forgotten behavior, may reveal more than our memories about our remotely former selves. In 1919 Freud gave the name "repetition-compulsion" to the human propensity to repeat behavior, and he used it to explain our sense of the uncanny.

> It must be explained that we are able to postulate the principle of a *repetition-compulsion* in the unconscious mind, based upon instinctual activity and probably inherent in the very nature of the instincts—a principle powerful enough to overrule the pleasure-principle, lending to certain aspects of the mind their daemonic character, and still very clearly expressed in the tendencies of small children; a principle, too, which is responsible for a part of the course taken by the analyses of neurotic patients. Taken in all, the foregoing prepares us for the discovery that whatever reminds us of this inner *repetition-compulsion* is perceived as uncanny.[21]

Though less popularly known, repetition-compulsion has been considered by some Freudians to be a third instinct, as important as the sexual and the self-destruction ones. It has been used to explain the *displacement* of affectionate and hostile feelings, from their previous focus upon parent or spouse, to the doctor–analyst during therapy. These emotional repetitions are sometimes called "pursuing fate," and "fate neurotic" is a label given to unfortunates who compulsively repeat destructive actions.[22] Compulsive repetition was also used by Freud to explain what, on his own principles, was puzzling; namely, that not all of our actions seem directed toward the reduction of tension or energy-arousal. Increase of sexual tension, for instance, is pleasurable and invites repetition.

Freud's principle was at work in the case of a young woman, told to us by a Boston psychiatrist. She married a medical student, supported him during his internship, and divorced him after he began practice. She later married another medical student, supported him during his internship, and divorced him after he began practice. After repeating this sequence a third time, she sought professional help. In repetition-compulsion, then, we come to see the "hidden cause" (the accumulation of past experience) of what we think ourselves to be doing freely. The young woman certainly believed, when she made them, that her repeated choices of medical students were not compelled but free.

In *Beyond the Pleasure Principle* (1919) Freud suggested that the repetition of behavior happily holds within a restricted scope of emotional stimulation such that self-control is at least possible. Without such repetition, the range of stimulation would be so indefinite that we could never identify ourselves in terms of an emotional and behavioral pattern capable of being understood and controlled.[23]

Evidence supporting the concepts of reinforcement and repetition-compulsion can create the suspicion that something in one's nature, due to the accumulation of certain experiences, is the "invisible" control over one's choices or decisions. The decision-making process is itself suspected to be caused, such that we *cannot decide* other than as we do in fact decide to act. If our decisions behind our actions are forced, so then are our actions. My dancing a jig is forced if my decision to do it is forced. Accordingly, the trust of common sense in the general freedom of human action is naïve unless the general freedom of human decision is assured.

Sometimes we experience a forced decision, when the urge to do something is felt as irresistible. We feel ourselves "swept" into the decision. In the absence of counterevidence, the experience is adequate evidence for declaring the decision compulsive. On the other hand, what we consciously experience or can introspect is often irrelevant in judging whether the decision was free or not. For example, a person posthypnotically obeying the hypnotist's instructions has no feeling of coercion, but his decision may indeed be outside his own control. Moreover, decisions or choices can strike us as more elusive, less well-defined, than actions. The process of "making up one's mind" can be hard to identify in detail. It can occur so quickly that it almost escapes notice. Also, we can be baffled by the manner in which our deliberatings and hesitatings will suddenly terminate, and then we decide to do something. Decision-making is often more difficult than action to control, less amenable to experimentation. Determining whether decisions are free can therefore look like a perplexing task. It may seem easier to judge whether actions are free or coerced—until we recall that freedom of action depends upon freedom of decision.

There is no dodging the distinction between decision and action. We do some things without deciding to do them, like sleepwalking, frowning, tapping a rhythm, and so on. And we may decide to do something but be prevented from doing it. Or consider a situation envisaged by John Locke (1632-1704): A man is carried into a room while asleep and locked inside. The man awakes, considers whether to stay or leave, and decides to stay, unaware that the door is locked and that he could not exit if he wanted to.[24] We say that the act of remaining in the room was compelled, though the man, in his ignorance, mistakenly believed he was acting freely. But his decision, we may presume, unless counterevidence is offered, was freely arrived at. His deciding to remain was not compelled (unless some hidden cause for it is revealed). That the decision was free does not insure that the act was free, though if the decision was compelled, then so was the act. That the act was free insures that the decision was free, though if the act was compelled, that the decision was also compelled is not insured.

To be sure, there are unanswered questions about the concept of decision-making and about the psychological details of arriving at a choice. Further, in particular cases the evidence as to whether the decision was free or compelled may be practically impossible to locate. But common sense will never abandon the conviction that our decisions are generally free, that we can choose or decide other than we do. And for excellent reasons! Again, as with actions, we only look for hidden causes that compel when the decisions are deviant or unusual, as with addicts and kleptomaniacs. In general (despite the lack of complete parallelism, as shown by Locke's example discussed earlier), action illustrates decision. We do not customarily decide freely to act compulsively, so Locke's locked-in man is in the exceptional predicament of freely choosing to do what he was compelled to do anyway, staying in the room. There is no evidence that we compulsively choose our usual or normal behavior. Evidence that our action is free is evidence that our deciding to do it is free; special counterevidence is needed before concluding differently.

It is totally a question of *evidence*. This is important. John Stuart Mill (1808–1873) and William James (1842–1910) sank into emotional quicksand worrying about whether human decision is ever really free. James said he survived through demonstrating his freedom to himself in deciding to believe in that freedom. We smile at this, knowing that decisions are not proof, demonstrations of conclusions. Yet James had the right hunch; his uncertainty about freedom was a paralysis needing not proof but decision. You think, maybe all decision is covertly compelled. You then ask, how can this thought be disproved? The answer—only by weighing the evidence. And we repeat, there is no evidence whatever that all human decision is compelled; the evidence is thoroughly against any such wild supposition. A persisting suspicion on behalf of compulsion is not refutable, because all appeal to evidence has been dismissed or forgotten. This suspicion can only be cured by deciding to return to the evidence. Philosophers learn something about motivation themselves—that decision can be more difficult than it looks.

Theories of motivation are not theories of compulsion. Theories of reinforcement are like theories in economics; they may predict quite accurately how people will behave under certain conditions, not because compelled, but because they freely will seek reinforcing (rewarding) stimuli as they will voluntarily look for the best buy. We can predict quite a lot, once we know what people want and will freely tend to do. Psychoanalysis offers numerous but untested explanations for what it calls "compulsive" behavior when it apparently occurs, but sometimes the theory appears itself impulsive in its indentification of compulsive behavior. It is odd that a woman repeats a marriage–divorce sequence three times, but evidence other than oddity is required to show that what she did was outside her control. Tendencies to repeat behavior are not *ipso facto* compulsive, and psychoanalytic employment of "repetition-compulsion" must always be checked against the evidence.

The new psycho-bio-chemico-anthro-physical alliance promises to tell us more about the sources of *aberrant* behavior. Spurred by ingenious techniques using the lessons of reinforcement theory, by new uses of RNA, etc., increases in *unusual* achievements should be scored by rats, pigeons, and humans. But we may already know all we need to know about what motivates us on an average day.[25]

6

Emotion and Feeling

The discussion of emotion has been about as confused as that of any topic in psychology, partly because the terminology is often equivocal and partly because tradition carries great weight in this part of the field and it is hard to keep a modern point of view consistently.

[D. O. Hebb, *Organization of Behavior*]

1. Some Theories

Philosophers once emphasized the distinction between Doing and Suffering, between Activity and Passivity. Emotions were subsumed under the latter category, because they were conceived as happenings rather than doings. The idea was that in action we take over, whereas in emotion we are taken over. We are active in doing, passive in feeling. The distinction obviously has some basis, but it can easily be exaggerated. For we can act passively, not from initiative but from habit or resignation. On the other hand, since we can actively encourage certain emotions in ourselves, we are sometimes less passive in relation to them than we are to certain of our actions.

One valuable point, which the traditional distinctions between doing and feeling may have intended, is that we can do some actions at will, at this moment if we wish, but we can rarely (perhaps never) turn on or off our emotions at will. You may justifiably accuse me of carelessly drifting into present seizures of anger and jealousy, but you cannot think me capable of obeying an order, on the instant, to eliminate them. Emotions are like lamps that automatically turn on at dusk and off at dawn. They are responses to specific circumstances, and we can control our emotional lives to the extent that we can identify and regulate the appropriate circumstances. Control of emotion is generally indirect. We prohibit or permit anger in ourselves by the steps we take, by the circumstances by which we allow ourselves to be surrounded. Generally, then, we control emotion through action, because action, far more than emotion, can be achieved at will.

Our interest in emotion can be aesthetic, in the felt details of the fear, the sexual arousal, the mounting anxiety, or it can be moral, in the emotion as laudable or culpable. But our interest is mostly practical or strategical. Since emotion motivates action, we naturally want control of emotion. It is often remembered that emotion is commotion, prolongation of which is usually intolerable. Our interest in emotions is generally negative, because most of them are unpleasant and easily provoke regrettable actions. A sample list makes the point: fear, anger, jealousy, anxiety, revulsion, grief, depression, joy, ecstasy, love, and heightened anticipation. Emotion tends to seek its own cessation through action, and we all know what it is like to be a bullied participant in the process. For many, having an emotional experience is like going to the dentist; the strategy is to undergo it rarely and in such a manner that it discourages its own repetition. For many, the most exquisite experience is the relief succeeding the expended emotion, also a release from the emotion's pressure to find outlet in unwanted action. This general verdict was apparently shared by Aristotle in his famous opinion that the value of watching tragic drama is in the psychological calm following "catharsis" of the emotions of pity and terror.

Dislike and distrust of most emotions are reflected in psychological theories that treat emotions as disorganized responses. But, as an assessment of *all* emotional experience, such a view seems clearly exaggerated. Predictably, therefore, other theories in psychology have been proposed to demonstrate that emotion contributes to the *organization* of personality and behavior. Studies by Darwin (1809–1882) on emotion may be cited for the claim that, while most emotions are perhaps signals of distress, some (joy and love, for instance) are surely symptoms of melodious adjustment. It is reassuring to find within professional psychology the Motivational Theory of emotion. For this theory rightly emphasizes the common sense conviction that emotions are not only (sometimes disruptive) responses to situations but also motivate action. It also reminds us that we can afford to think more optimistically about emotion, insofar as it occasionally motivates beneficial behavior.[1]

Professional and popular opinion on the causal role of emotions, it should be noted, can and do clash. Probably the most startling of all professional declarations was by William James, when he said that we do not really cry because we are sad or run because we are afraid, but rather we are sad because we cry and are afraid because we run.[2] This is of course an indefensible generalization, as James himself eventually conceded. What he was in fact arguing is that our emotions are dependent upon our bodily processes and behavior. Sometimes (though not always) if you walk downheartedly, you will soon feel dejected; if you walk smartly, you will soon feel chipper, and so on. The bodily processes of which our emotions are functions, James thought, are not exclusively centralized brain states but include, as well, what is happening throughout the entirety of one's body.[3] James did not intend to deny that actions are often the effects of emotions. His target was rather a dualistic theory of mind and body, which conceived of emotions as capable of occurring "pure and unconnected" with the body. His point was that anger, say, is *physiological* commotion, and that such an emotion might exist apart from such physiological commotion is unthinkable. The point is now taken for granted and is the unquestioned assumption of all current research into the biochemical foundations of emotion.

But James had to abandon his challenge of common sense on the motivational capacity of emotion. We do, of course, cry *because* we are sad, run *because* we are afraid. However, according to current distinguished philosophical opinion, while this is true and James was wrong, it does not mean what you may think it does. You may conclude (mistakenly), whenever it is true that a person acts "because of a certain emotion," that the person's action is due to his being overcome by an emotional *experience*. Thus, if Jones jumped from fear, then his jumping was caused by his feeling or experiencing fear. But the "then" does not follow from the "if" here, for this reason: Saying that Jones jumped from fear may mean, not that he experienced fear, but rather that, being habitually a fearful person, he was already disposed to jump in startling circumstances. When we say that Jones acts because of fear, we may be noting how he habitually acts or is ready to act in special circumstances, without neces- sarily attributing to him a certain emotional experience at the time.

The point is important. So very often we declare ourselves and others to have acted out of fear, anger, jealousy, vanity, etc. It is a question of evidence, beyond the mere declaration, whether, on a specific occasion, the action was caused by an emotional experience or is the manifestation of a habit. I cannot infer, just because "I struck from anger" is colloquially true, that my action was caused by an overpowering feeling of anger. Further evidence is required to substantiate the latter claim. It may be that, rather than excusing my action on the basis of an alleged uncontrollable experience of anger, I really need to hold myself responsible for habitually acting angrily (even in the absence of angry feelings).[4]

The foregoing can mitigate, without resolving, another possi- ble clash between professional and popular thinking about emotion. Psychoanalysis does not question the motivational capacity of emotion. But it says a good deal, often in puzzling fashion, about our susceptibility to self-deception about our emotions. It insists that we are often self-deceived about our real emotions in our relations, say, with parents and siblings. Though we think we love them, we in fact somewhat hate them. And psychoanalysts intimate, not simply that we misunderstand our real emotions, but that we are "unconscious" of them. We may find this puzzling, on the grounds that, whereas an *unconscious emotional experience* might be thought to occur rarely, it seems incredible to suppose that emotions of anger and jealousy can often happen without one's awareness of them. Popular belief may thus suspect the psychoanalytic claim that we are self-deceived about much of our emotional life insofar as we are "unconscious" of it.

But some reconciliation results when we recall the point previously made; namely, that much talk about emotions is actually more about behavior than about something felt or experienced. Psychoanalysts tell their patients that they are behaving out of anxiety, hate, or resentment. The patients sometimes reply that they do not remember having *felt* the emotions associated with anxiety, hate, or resentment. The analysts reply that the emotions are real though unnoticed, because they are in the patients' unconscious. One can argue here that, for such psychoanalysts, felt emotions are apparently quite *unimportant*. It is the behavior-pattern that is significant. What patients need to learn about themselves is that their behavior-patterns, in relation to parents and siblings, strikingly resemble those of people who actively hate their close relatives and who also strongly feel the emotions associated with hating. What the patient is "unconscious" of is the pattern of his behavior, in the sense that he fails to realize how it can be persuasively diagnosed. What he misunderstands is how he typically behaves, how that looks to others. Thus, we need not endorse the puzzling statement that he is unconscious of feelings of anxiety, hate, and resentment in the sense that he literally fails to notice such *commotional* feelings as they occur. To this extent, we may placate popular sentiment, without, however, attempting to decide whether emotions and feelings *ever* do occur unnoticed.[5]

Classical or Freudian psychoanalysis is not always clear in its remarks on emotion, whether it is behavior or feeling that is paramount. Certain psychoanalytic theorists may have this in mind when observing that there is no systematic treatment of emotion in Freud.[6] Freudian literature can leave one unsure about the emphases. Is it coming to feel a repressed emotion or rather remembering a traumatic experience in childhood that is more important? Is it learning to introspect one's own experience or rather coming to share the analyst's diagnosis of one's behavior-pattern that is really significant? Other theorists and therapists have declared their emphases. The Existentialists respect the minutest introspective reports of their patients. Every nuance of the person's experience is of utmost importance.[7] Therapists, who see their patients as a group rather than alone, employ techniques to make one feel, maybe for the first time, what has long been smouldering below the surface. Feeling, not diagnosis of past behavior, is here the dividend. In contrast, neo-Freudian literature on emotion seems to focus more on assimilating emotions into the architectonic of Freudian theory. This is a highly abstract endeavor, quite remote from popular concern with emotion. In this respect Freudian theory resembles much theorizing in academic psychology about emotion, where the primary interest is often less in the emotions themselves than it is in the formal status of the concept of emotion within either some psychological theory or some theory about psychology.[8]

2. Emotions and Feelings

It is time to distinguish between emotions and feelings, because not all of what has been and will be said about the one is true of the other. Since there is no standard distinction in psychology, we can only offer our own. All emotions are, we suggest, *in part* feelings, but not all feelings are even in part emotions. We therefore reject the following: ". . . *an emotion may be defined as a patterned bodily reaction of either destruction, reproduction, incorporation, orientation, protection, deprivation, rejection, or exploration, or some combination of these, which is brought about by a stimulus.*"[9]

This is really a definition of certain types of *emotional behavior*. We have agreed previously that emotional behavior can occur in the absence of emotional feelings (i.e., emotions). But, when we speak of emotions rather than emotional actions, we refer to something *felt*. The emotion called "anger," say, is partly a feeling with which most of us are acquainted. It is also an impulse or readiness to strike, to hurt, to shout, and so on. It is not merely a feeling; but it is also not merely behavior, as the above definition would have it.

It is always sensible to ask how an emotion feels. Investigators report that college students describe the feeling of fear as unpleasant, tense, contracted; whereas love is felt as pleasant, relaxed, expansive. Anger is felt as active, tense and rough. How does grief feel? It is sad, tense, cold and weak. And pride? It is high, active, clear, full, and loud. That the descriptions are largely metaphorical is unimportant. What matters is that they are appropriate responses to the question, How does it (the emotion) feel? But, though it sounds odd, one can also ask how a feeling feels. You can be queried, for instance, as to whether your feeling of dizziness is unpleasant or pleasant. This is not the same as asking for a description of the dizziness, so describing a feeling and describing how it feels are evidently different things. But we cannot sensibly ask how the feelings of pleasantness and unpleasantness feel; hence, the unusual position sometimes accorded these feelings in psychology texts is justified. They are the two exceptions, among feelings, in being distinguishable from emotions by virtue of the fact that the question of how they feel cannot be asked of them.

Feelings are less commotional than emotions. Since it is a difference in degree, the distinction can only be drawn roughly. Feelings are less turbulent than emotions. Less bodily tension and fewer bodily sensations attend the feeling of satisfaction than characterize the emotion of ecstasy. Quieter than emotions are the feelings of accomplishment, of sympathy, of doubt, of tranquillity, of boredom, of finality, of cheerfulness, of wistfulness, of tenderness, and so on. We intend this distinction when contrasting the feeling and the emotion of disappointment, the feeling and the emotion of annoyance, the feeling and the emotion of anticipation, etc. Some feelings, like that of dizziness, more closely approach emotional status.

Feelings are, in general, subtler experiences than emotions. Whether a feeling can occur totally unnoticed will not be debated here. It is surely evident, however, that feelings may virtually escape our attention, that they may occur ignored by us, unappreciated and unattended to in the flux of experience. Passing in and out of our experience, often virtually overlooked and forever forgotten, are quiet feelings of appreciation, tenderness, faint disappointment, admiration, disapproval, satisfaction, dissatisfaction, expectancy, withdrawal, expansiveness, regret, sympathy, concern, worry, puzzlement, tranquillity, affection, success, failure, righteousness, pride, envy, depression, self-rejection, curiosity, and so on. And bodily feelings associated with sitting, standing, breathing, etc., or with slight changes in temperature, or with changes in perception, and so on. People find all emotion too pronounced and most of it too unpleasant to be able to ignore it. Its connection with emotional behavior is too intimate to permit indifference, whereas the very modesty of much feeling consigns it to oblivion.

Feelings are the aesthetic content of introspective experience. They can be attended to and savored for their own sake. Unlike emotions, they do not demand behavioral outlet. They are not of obvious practical significance, nor is introspection; accordingly, people tend not to introspect nor to savor feelings. Like a still life on the wall of a hectic office, or a melody in a noisy cocktail lounge, most feeling is in the background of a busy, practical attention. Tarrying on a feeling of accomplishment gets you nowhere, and who, save a pervert like Dostoyevsky's underground man, could possibly be led to dwell with relish on the feelings of envy and resentment?

This opinion of feelings, however, is profoundly mistaken. First, though feelings do not typically provoke actions, and to this extent are not practically significant, they are immensely important in shaping personality, for feelings underlie attitudes. Our personalities are not only the products of our deeds, as a tradition extending from Aristotle to Jean Paul Sartre has insisted. They are also formed out of feelings. You can become a coward by repeated acts of cowardice, but you can likewise reach that end by permitting the recurrence of cowardly feelings to go unattended and unchecked. Secondly, if ignored and left to themselves, feelings tend to cluster on the principle that "like seeks like." The feeling of indifference can invite the feeling of futility, which joins with that of resignation, and so on. Thus, thirdly, introspective attention to such feelings is important; to note the strength of those feelings, the degree of their recurrence, the tendency of their associations, etc. Such attention may provide a basis for their alleviation or elimination. Fourthly, desirable feelings may need cultivating; neglected, they wither on the vine. In the case of feelings, a tendency to recur is a normal response to approving attention. The importance of this is obvious, once we recall how our possession of desirable attitudes largely depends upon our experiencing desirable feelings.

Our discussion has proceeded on the premiss that we can come to know the nature of our feelings and emotions, that we can learn to identify and classify them. We have perhaps left the impression that becoming acquainted with our feelings and emotions is a straightforward affair. In practice, people find that it is not. Requested to identify or articulate their present feelings, they may respond hesitantly and confusedly. This fact we need to look at further.

3. Knowing Our Feelings

The most important fact about feelings is that they form attitudes. You have a better chance of being a sympathetic person if you are prone to feelings of sympathy, of being a contrite person if prone to feelings of contrition, an irritable individual if feelings of irritation, a gleeful person if feelings of glee, and so on. Perhaps the most important fact about feelings is that they seem often elusive and hard to pin down for identification. This is not always true of course. When feeling annoyed, sad, appreciative, affectionate, etc., there may be no sense of elusiveness about the feeling nor doubt about how to label it. Feelings *can* be as frank as one could wish.

But also consider: If you are suddenly asked how or what you are feeling, you may feel taken by surprise and at a loss for an answer. Unless you have been aware of some pronounced feeling, you will probably say something like, "nothing in particular." You may actually be impressed by the fact that you seem to be feeling nothing whatever. It is like having your friend request your response to his abstract painting, and you find that you have no response, but, if subsequently you do, you wonder whether you "manufactured" it for the occasion. But you may think it queer, upon reflection, that you feel nothing at all. It is uncomfortably close to confessing to being a vegetable. So could you possibly be overlooking some feelings? This question becomes more haunting by virtue of the fact that under guided questioning you *become* aware of feelings. Asked how your foot feels, you begin to note feelings in your foot. Asked about your frame of mind, you realize that a feeling of sadness or satisfaction swims into attention. Queried about the effect of my questioning, you realize that you have been feeling resentful. Asked about the wart on the chap's nose you were staring at, you record a feeling of disgust. You now marvel at the elusiveness of your feelings, which can only be captured through our combined efforts.

Then there is the problem of identification and description. You can know that you are feeling something but not know what to call it or how to characterize it. Is it a feeling of sympathy or rather one of empathy?[10] Is it annoyance or rather disgust? Remorse or dejection? Satisfaction or relief? Is "expansive" or "vital" the better adjective for it? Or are no simple adjectives adequate, rather requiring a whole phrase or paragraph to convey it? And, even after that, you may not quite trust the description. Possibly another phrasing would get at the feeling better. Or maybe all language must fail somewhat, there always remaining a residue of unarticulated feeling?

We might summarize the foregoing in terms of a contrast.

We look out and behold a well-defined scene—streets, cars, trees, buildings, and so on. We can run and rerun our eyes over the scene in noting more and more details, but when we turn to look at the "inner scene" of feelings, it seems hazy, shadowy, jungled. There does not seem even to be a "scene" to be reexamined for details. Now and then feelings move clearly into view, but most of them form a thicket too dense to permit discrete identifications.

But, say some philosophers, our wanting to make such a contrast in itself reveals how we have really created a batch of pseudoperplexities about feelings. It shows that we are mistakenly thinking of feelings as being comparable to things seen, observed, looked at. It is nonsensical, they hold, to talk of "observing" feelings. A person can be asked whether he "has" a certain feeling, but he cannot be asked, except ridiculously, whether he "observes" it. Accordingly, if feelings are thought of as akin to objects of vision, no wonder they "look" so hazy! For indeed you cannot see what cannot be seen.

Nevertheless, even if to speak of "observing" feelings is misleading, we properly speak of "noting," "attending to," "dwelling upon" them. The analogy with vision is not wholly misleading; for the awareness of feelings is to some degree capable of regulation and modification, such that feelings can be apprehended with varying degrees of vividness. Its duration is often controllable, and "in depth" introspection can sometimes indicate how the feeling is best described. But the analogy with visual awareness is misleading, if it encourages us to suppose that we can smoothly transmute the vocabulary of vision into a vocabulary of feeling. Describing a feeling as "expansive" is initially metaphorical, and borrowed from the vocabulary of sight. If one then wonders, on occasion, whether "expansive" best fits a certain feeling, the old rules for its use will not suffice for a decision. It becomes necessary to develop guidelines for its new role in the vocabulary of feeling. The language of sight is richer than that pertaining to any other sense, because for most of us the visual world is the practical one. Odors, tastes, sounds, etc., are mainly of aesthetic interest, and, consequently, their languages are like the language of feeling in being less developed. On an elementary level, we know what we mean by borrowing from one language to another. We know the basis for speaking of "hot" colors, "cool" sounds, "big" feelings, and so on; but, as we make our descriptions more sophisticated and more searching, such borrowings can make us uncertain about those descriptions. Are they "manufactured," or do they report the feeling? Would another description better suit the feeling? This then is the first point, that some uncertainty about identifying and describing feelings is due to our having to create a language for that purpose. This is just a hard fact about experience. Such uncertainty is not spurious but has a real basis.

Uncertainty increases with the demand for increased precision of description. Introspection of a routine sort can decide whether I am annoyed or not. But if I am pressed to be more exact, to specify whether the annoyance is more like anger than disappointment, whether it more resembles what occurs when a student corrects me than what occurs when a colleague does, whether it is like what I would experience if my dog has a litter of two rather than four puppies, I become less confident how to answer. When identifying the feeling requires comparisons involving recollections and predictions, routine introspection no longer suffices; but it is not therefore irrelevant, as philosophers sometimes conclude. Introspection can always provide a vague, minimal characterization of the feeling. When I reduce the vagueness by comparing it to a feeling formerly experienced or to a hypothetical one in the future, then the accuracy of my description is a function of my ability to recollect and to predict. This then is our second point, that we must be prepared to accept greater uncertainty about our descriptions of feeling when we make them more specific and detailed.

Now it should be noted that philosophers and psychologists rarely discuss *this* or *that* feeling. They leave that kind of discussion to poets, dramatists, and Aunt Sadie. They have been interested, not in this or that feeling or emotion, but in classes or kinds of feelings and emotions. Some thought that one class might be defined in terms of another, thus developing the distinction between primary and secondary emotions. Descartes argued, for instance, that all other emotions could be understood in terms of six primary ones—love, joy, admiration, desire, hatred, and sadness. Spinoza reduced the primary ones to three—joy, sorrow, and desire. Hobbes (1588–1679) thought these primary: appetite, love, grief, desire, aversion, joy, and hate. McDougall (1871–1938) carried on this tradition of defining one kind of emotion in terms of another.[11] Presumably, these theorists would have applied the primary–secondary distinction to feelings as well as to emotions.

Spinoza undoubtedly believed that he was clarifying the concepts of love and hatred in saying, "Love is nothing but joy accompanied with the idea of an external cause, and hatred is nothing but sorrow with the accompanying idea of an external cause." Fear, he said, is "an unsteady sorrow, arising from the image of a doubtful thing." Remorse is "that sorrow which is opposed to gladness," and pride is "that joy which arises from a man's thinking too much of himself."[12] These observations are certainly suggestive, possessing the sort of illumination peculiar to epigrams, but they are not improvements in precision of description. That purpose is not obtained by comparing kinds of emotions with each other, or by thinking of emotions as mixtures or blends of each other.[13] In talking about remorse, one remains there in comparing it to sorrow. One must ask, what specific version of remorse under what specific circumstances is being compared to what specific version of sorrow, in what specific situations? I pin down the "introspectible feel" of an experience to the extent that I can compare it in detail with that of other experiences. I must ask, is it like the remorse I felt when I slipped or when I slapped, or like the sorrow I felt when I retched or when I ratted? We elaborate the introspectible feel of an experience by citing the contents of its occurrences. This, we saw, requires accuracy of recall and prediction, causing some uncertainty about our more elaborate descriptions of our feelings. But learning to specify feelings in terms of specific comparisons is highly important. It makes us aware of those feelings that recur, those that occur only rarely, under what circumstances they are likely to happen, and so on. It is essential to knowing our feelings. Moreover, it is a necessary part of learning to take a more active interest in the life of feeling, of being more attentive to the opportunities for feeling.[14]   This brings us to the third and final point about uncertainty and feeling. A good share of feeling is a function of interest, of attention. If you are interested in the back of your neck, attend to it, you will probably feel various things there. If you are interested in how the lady's words affect you, attend to it, you will probably become aware of certain feelings. Feelings are generally elusive insofar as we allow our opportunities for experiencing them to elude us. The issue is not only whether feelings occur unconsciously but whether we allow them to happen and whether we take an interest in them when they do. Feeling is blocked by distraction, shifting interest, divided attention. Most of the uncertainty that declares feelings highly elusive is the uncertainty of distraction. If so, it is not only through overt action that we can control our feelings and, derivatively, some of our basic attitudes. We can also accomplish that in some degree by taking the proper interest and devoting the required attention.[15]

7

Fantasy

1. Imagination

The topic of imagination has always engaged philosophers. Their speculations about the relations between imagination and intellect foreshadowed psychological theories about the connections between imagination and insight. They defined imagination as the capacity to be aware of images, the kind of thing one attends to when dreaming, hallucinating, daydreaming, etc. Plato's concept of imagination became a tradition in Western thought. Imagination serves the soul and helps the mind to think, according to Plato, but it really belongs more to the body. For instance, images and illustrations may help you to learn mathematics; you may need them in learning the concept of a point or the concept of a circle. But when you learn what mathematics means by "point," you learn that it is purely abstract, has no spatial dimensions, and therefore cannot in all accuracy be represented by images or graphic illustrations that do possess spatial dimensions. Images are consequently inferior to pure thoughts. Plato and Descartes both observed that what can be thought may not be imaginable. You can conceive of a thousand-sided figure, Descartes noted, but you cannot imagine it. They also believed that imagination dies with the body, whereas pure thought survives as the activity of the soul.

The tradition was challenged, notably in eighteenth-century British philosophy, by thinkers who concluded that "pure thoughts" and "abstract ideas" were myths. They tried to show how images can do all that was formerly assigned to pure thoughts. Every important debate ever held about imagination has been revived in the twentieth century. Some hold that pure or imageless thought occurs, while others deny that they can even understand the claim. Others declare that usual accounts of imagining and dreaming are oddly mistaken, and there is no need to assume an "inner theater" of images in explaining what it is to imagine or to dream. An opposed position is represented by Bertrand Russell, who has written that images are the *only* things that are mental rather than physical. The limitations of imagination, as the awareness of images, have been emphasized in the philosophy of science. What can be conceived in the mathematical language of physics may not be picturable, the states of affairs postulated by quantum mechanics being a case in point. On the other hand, some contend, the imaginable is not always expressible; no language, including the language of physics, can quite express what we sometimes imagine. The richness of imagery, they say, is unmatched by any language.

These are interesting issues, and we comment on certain of them in other chapters. Our purpose in this chapter, however, is to move the topic of imagination closer to current work in psychology, psychiatry, and psychoanalysis.

2. Fantasy

We have chosen fantasy as our titular word here, not because we intend to press a special distinction between fantasy and imagination, but because we want to emphasize that our interest in the topic of imagination is not in the traditional philosophical mold. We are interested in the imaginary insofar as it is at once philosophically and psychoanalytically significant. Fantasies may be experiences like daydreams, or they may be obsessive attitudes or beliefs that are curiously unrealistic. These may be both philosophically and psychoanalytically significant.

A severe fantasy, like imagining that one is being chased by a menacing crayfish, is an hallucination. Believing that one is Napoleon or Cleopatra is psychotic. Some fantasies are fortunately milder, like imagining that one is a great artist, athlete, or lover, and are neither hallucinatory nor psychotic. Some beliefs, which have been called "philosophical" and which have fascinated the popular imagination, are possibly mild fantasies. The belief that "all is one" is perhaps an example. That "nothing changes" or that "everything changes" is another example. That "one's fate is in the stars" is another. That "time is unreal" and "the visible world is a veil" are others. Perhaps also is the belief that "humans are essentially good" or that "humans are basically bad." But we must be cautious here. We do not claim that such beliefs are always mild fantasies. We say that they can be of that sort for people whose minds are attached to them in special ways, adding the supporting note that beliefs, which are sometimes called "philosophical" and which occasionally fascinate the popular imagination, are where many minds do get stuck in special ways.[1]

Individuals sometimes declare that they cannot help thinking that the world is only a veil. Or they may say that they have a nagging hunch that everyone is basically selfish. Some may claim that an unusual experience taught them that everything is really one. Beyond noting how unrealistic are these "philosophical" beliefs, it is perhaps pointless to debate their merits. It is possibly more worthwhile to discover *why* someone is drawn to them, why he finds them difficult to lay aside. It can be important to uncover the psychoanalysis in his philosophy. Why does he want to believe it? Why is he afraid of disbelieving it? Why is he unable to bring himself to another way of thinking? Why is he content to mull the logic of the fantastic?

Hopefully, we have now conveyed the nature of our concern in this chapter. It is, however, more focused than has been indicated thus far. We have our eye on one particular "philosophical fantasy," for the confrontation of which the next section will prepare us.

3. Fantasies and Body-Image

The word "image" is widely employed. There is the image of himself that a person sees in the mirror; there is the different sort of image of himself that he sees in dreams; there is the different kind of image of himself that he has when ascribing to himself a certain type of personality; there is also the image of himself that he projects in causing others to ascribe to him a certain type of personality; and there is the image that he has of himself in terms of what he thinks he can and ought to be. Psychologists have recently added to the list the image a person has of his own body, and they call this "body-image."

Since Sir Henry Head's celebrated studies of neurology and aphasia in the 1920's a vast amount of literature has been steadily accumulating on the concept of body-image. The concept is diversely interpreted, and few writers agree on the meaning of "body-image." Some prefer other terms, including "body-schema," "postural schema," "image of the body-ego," "body-percept," "somato-psyche," and "somatognosia." The following meanings have been attached to these terms: the way one feels about one's own body, the kind of postural awareness that one has of one's body in standing upright or in other positions, a kind of awareness of the parts of the body in their relations to each other, a sense of one's body-as-a-whole, a literal image of one's body, a kind of image-map that one has of one's body. What is often emphasized is that one's image of one's own body may be curiously off the mark, and that if one's normal image of one's body is altered or damaged, strange results occur. Though the concept is vague indeed, let us settle here for saying that your "body-image" is a kind of picture you have of your body and one that is infused with attitudes, positive and negative. It is your pictorial attitude toward your own body.[2]

Your relation to your body is uniquely personal, and how you picture it and what your attitude is toward it obviously affect your whole being. Your attitude toward your body can be quite tyrannical, requiring you to move in a "little boy" or "little girl" way, to move jerkily, to stand in a slouch, and so on. Ask a girl in a dance class to move aggressively, chin out and arms up with elbows jutting to the sides, with a twist through the hips, and she may burst into tears, protesting that she *cannot* do it. Her physical abilities and motor coordination may be entirely adequate, yet she *feels* that she cannot do it, so we naturally conclude that she has a mental block. In investigating this, we may find various reasons. It may be that her body-image is soft and lyrical, and she cannot imagine yanking her delicate self into aggressive posturing. Or it may be that she has difficulty in picturing, without the constant aid of mirrors, what aggressive movements are on herself; so, when she thinks that she is acting aggressively, she is in fact only repeating, with slight modifications, her usual lyrical movements. Or it may be that she is suspicious that you are trying to get her to reveal a side of herself, an angry and short-tempered disposition, which she anxiously wants to conceal. And so on.[3]

Your body is your presentation of yourself to the world, and naturally, therefore, you will necessarily hold your own body in a special light. It is interesting, for example, that psychologists have confirmed that, when people *unknowingly* respond to pictures of their own bodies, they express more emotion than they do when reacting to pictures of other people. The problems experienced by art students in doing self-portraits testify to the same point.

It appears that one's body-image, in some of its aspects, crystallizes early. One begins, in childhood, to favor certain areas of his body while disfavoring others. We can deny parts of the body so intensely that they go virtually umperceived. How fearful or anxious we feel about our bodies is often a

function of childhood experience. Adult men who prefer intellectual to athletic activity are often found to have experienced
body-anxiety as youngsters. Current research aims at more
specific results, in explaining how one's body-image develops,
and analyzing body-image into its more specific dimensions.
Various techniques, including word associations, drawings,
responses to ink blots, and tachistoscopically presented pictures,
are being used to determine these more specific dimensions of
body-image, including the following: anxiety about one's body,
displeasure with one's body, estimation of one's bodily propor-
tions, plasticity of body scheme, sense of one's position in space,
comparative evaluation of left and right body sides, and associations of gender with certain bodily parts. Investigations
suggest that an individual's image of his bodily size correlates
with his ability to make independent judgments, with his
tendency toward personality integration or disorganization,
with the kind of exposure experienced to sensory isolation, and
with the ingestion of certain drugs. It has been found that
dramatic experiences of change in image of body size connect
with migraine attacks, development of transference in psychoanalytic therapy, and brain disorders. There seems to be a
"basic tendency for body feelings to be translated into body
size terms. The individual seems to register the many alterations
in his body feelings as shifts up and down a scale of small-
ness–bigness." [4]

Changes in body-image that are accompanied by significant
psychological changes are often caused by brain lesions (especially in the parietal lobes). A patient suffering from such a
lesion may raise his right arm only when told to raise both
arms. He is unaware of not having raised his left arm; yet, when
told of this, he may immediately lift his left arm, showing that
he still retains the motor ability. A patient may neglect one half
of his body, entirely unaware of this while bathing, dressing,
combing hair, applying cosmetics, etc. Objects on the neglected
side of this patient may also be completely unnoticed by him.
Tactile and auditory stimuli also fail to register on that side,
and a stimulus, besides being inadequately registered, may be

incorrectly located, being projected into a corresponding part of the body-half which is noticed. A hemiplegic patient (suffering loss of voluntary movements affecting one half of his body) may be unaware of his paralysis; he seems puzzled when his doctor refers to his affliction. His mental state is such that he is constantly prepared to deny that he is paralyzed, and, if it is pressed upon him that he is so afflicted, he shrugs it off with some wild, irrelevant explanation that still fails to acknowledge the fact. Or the patient may move an unparalyzed limb while thinking that he has moved the paralyzed one. He may even deny that the paralyzed limb is *his*. "The patient now becomes entangled in the web of a veritable delusional system. Thus, if the examiner follows up these statements rejecting ownership by some such question as 'Then whose limbs are these?,' the patient may assert that the limbs are those of some other person, fancied or real, alive or dead."[5] And some patients personify their paralyzed limbs, treating them as pets, playthings, or personalities, calling them by amusing nicknames.

Another dimension of body-image known as "body-boundary" has been studied distinctively by Seymour Fisher and Sidney Cleveland. Most of us presumably know our bodily boundaries, where our bodies terminate and the environment begins. We do not confuse the end of our nose with the icing on the cake that we stare at, but schizophrenics and brain-damaged patients may fail to discern whether certain stimuli originate outside or within their bodily boundaries. Normal people differ in how they experience their bodies as related to the environment, differing in the "definiteness or articulation" that they ascribe to the boundary areas of their bodies. Fisher and Cleveland have devised an index, called a barrier score, to assess the degree of a person's "boundary-definiteness." This index "equals the number of responses elicited by an ink blot series (e.g. Rorschach or Holtzman) that are characterized by an emphasis upon the protective, containing, decorative, or covering functions of the periphery."[6] The degree of definiteness that a person attaches to his bodily periphery is indicated by what he "sees" in the ink blot—"cave with rocky walls, person covered with a blanket, woman in fancy costume, mummy wrapped up, animal with striped skin, vase." By such techniques these investigators determine how well- or ill-defined people feel their bodily boundaries to be against the environment. They claim that not only is this interesting in itself, but that it is a symptom of other facts. For example, a person whose body-image is ill-defined at the boundaries, who accordingly "fantasizes" to a greater extent his bodily relation to the environment, will probably be more dependent, less motivated, less communicative, and so on. Whereas the definite-boundaried person tends to experience his bodily sensations in the skin and muscles, the indefinite-boundaried individual tends to feel them interiorly, in the heart and stomach.

People vary in how *vulnerable* they feel their bodies to be. Some may feel their bodily surfaces to be soft, porous, and even vulnerable to penetration by space itself; whereas others enjoy a body-image that is hard and resilient at the boundaries. Such people feel greater protection in their bodies. They move their bodies more like Buicks than Volkswagens. This dimension of body-image varies with circumstances. After a period of sensory isolation, a group of nonpsychotics displayed a sense of greater boundary vulnerability, whereas a group of schizophrenics showed just the reverse. How realistic or how "fantastic" we are in our feeling about our body relative to the environment depends, then, upon various factors affecting our body-images.

4. Self and Body-Image

The preceding discussion of body-image is philosophically significant. It is relevant to the topic of Chapter One, the philosophical concept of the self. We can appreciate, given the kind of information sampled in the preceding section, how oddities or distortions in one's body-image produce fantasies not only about one's body but also about one's total self. Fantasies about the nature of one's bodily boundaries are also fantasies about one's self. As one psychologist has written, "The

individual who views himself clearly and marks himself off
distinctly from persons and events of his environment is one
who can describe distinct events, persons, and sequences in his
fantasies."[7] Clearly, one's concept of self, of one's identity and
personality, is intimately affected by the fantasies produced by
oddities in one's body-image. If bodily identity tends to dissolve
in fantasy, so does self-identity.

The expression "body-image" is admittedly vague and invites
numerous questions about its use. Clarifying the concept, like
clarifying the concepts of drive, motivation, emotion, thought,
imagination, sensation, perception, knowledge, belief, memory,
etc., is a challenging task for philosophical psychology. Leaving
it here in the vagueness characteristic of its use in psychology
is due not to despair of achieving further clarification, but
rather to a desire to move to our main interest, and we believe
that the concept of body-image is at least sufficiently grasped
now to do that.

Distortions and oddities in body-image produce experiences
relevant to what we may call "the philosophical fantasy of
dualism." When the belief that oneself is a twofold entity, a
wedding of the body and a nonbodily thing (mind, soul, etc.),
is thought to be both suggested and justified by certain kinds
of experiences, we are tempted to describe that belief as a mild
fantasy. That temptation increases if the belief becomes at all
obsessive, if the belief is declared, for instance, to debar any
alternative mode of thinking on the grounds that certain
experiences make it that way. According to the testimony of
many people, their belief in the dualistic nature of the human
being is not based upon philosophical arguments or upon
scriptured authority but rather upon the intimations of special
experiences. Consider the following report of an individual's
recent experience induced by the drug mescaline.

> A majestic Beethoven chord exploded inside my brain, and
> I instantly disappeared. My body no longer existed, and neither
> did the world. The world and I had been utterly annihilated.
> I could feel the pressure of the earphones; but in the space
> between the phones, where my head should have been, there
> was absolutely nothing . . . nothing! I was mind alone, lost

in an icy blue grotto of sound. . . . The music rolled on in
orgiastic waves of sound and color, and then I myself was one
of the notes. I was being swept along on the silver staff, at twice
the speed of light, rushing farther and farther away from my
home back there in the Milky Way. In desperation, at the last
possible moment, I reached up with hands I did not own, and
I tore off the earphones.[8]

And this:

I could see myself from head to foot as well as the sofa on
which I was lying. About me was nothingness, absolutely
empty space. I was floating on a solitary island in the ether . . . .
The sofa island disappeared. I did not feel any physical self;
an ever increasing sense of dissolution set in, I was seized
with passionate curiosity, great things were about to be un-
veiled before me. I would perceive the essence of all things,
the problem of creation would be unraveled. I was demate-
rialized.[9]

Experiences like these can suggest the image of the body as
a sort of *container* of one's self. One's body-image becomes the
image of the body as a sort of envelope in which one lives.
Such experiences can provoke one to think that one's self looks
at the surrounding world from *within* the bodily container or
envelope; in rare situations, one even seems capable of slipping
outside the bodily container and, from outside, of gazing at
the container spread out on the sofa. In dreams one may seem
to see oneself as another person, and this can encourage the
image of one's body as the self's container. These are experiences
in which people *feel as if* they are not identical with their bodies,
in which they feel as if their bodies were things they move in
and out of. Given the image of the body as a kind of container,
the types of boundary-qualities characterizing it become psychoanalytically important. But this is fantasy, albeit a prevalent
one in Western culture, and one that has been defended by
elaborate argument.

The fantasy vaguely assumes that your body only "contains"
your real self, that it is not essential to the personality that you
are or to the emotional states that are yours. But consider: You
cannot in fact conceive of what it would be, to be still essentially
you, and at the same time to show disgust or admiration with

a totally different set of eyes, to smile your affection with another's mouth, to feel your anger rising in a chest twice yours in size, to scold your children from an eight-foot or three-foot height, to extend in love arms four times heavier than your present ones, to speak your usual intimacies in a voice suddenly gone soprano or baritone, to look in the same way at the world from a head that is permanently tilted. You cannot in fact conceive of the personality that you are being contained intact by the body of Frank Sinatra, George Wallace, or Margot Fonteyn.[10]

Philosophical dualism, which holds that the human being is a nonbodily self somehow contained in the body, asks us to grasp the idea that we could be the full-fledged personalities that we are without our present bodies or without bodies at all. But this request is so bewildering that we come to appreciate why religions are prudent in teaching that personal survival is bodily resurrection as well, and why, as some psychoanalysts have remarked half-seriously, the notion of disembodied survival must be of masculine origin, since no woman could find any logic in it. Even the authors of "esoteric" literature appear perplexed by philosophical dualism. For these authors, in their accounts of "out-of-the-body" experiences, give implicity or explicity *another* kind of body to the self emancipated from its ordinary set of limbs. Their description makes it plain that they, like us, cannot really conceive of personality except in terms of some kind of bodily expression. The fantasy that peculiar experiences can provoke is, therefore, not so much philosophical dualism but rather the thought that one's ordinary body is not the self's only and most effective body. For many esoteric minds, unlike philosophical dualism, *this* seems an *imaginable* hypothesis.

What evidently impresses individuals experiencing the effects of drugs like LSD, like what has always impressed those undergoing "mystical" experiences, are spectacular changes in body-image. It may suddenly seem weightless, its edges become blurred, it collapses and feels rubbery, and it even seems to "dematerialize" completely. The testimony of individuals experiencing the effects of drugs is of this sort. If the fantasy is extreme, if the individual is totally deluded or deranged, it is then pointless to ask how good a description he has given of his experience. He is in no position to check his words against his experience, so his testimony is worthless. He cannot distinguish between fantasy and delusion, much less fantasy and reality. The way he speaks can be a clue to his condition: If he speaks agitatedly, in panic or in ecstasy, saying not "I feel as if I'm dematerializing" but rather "I *am* dematerializing," he is probably in a very deranged state, and we are left in doubt about the relation between what he may be actually experiencing and his belief (that he is dematerializing) about what he is experiencing.

But when a person's sanity remains, and he knows that what he is experiencing is fantasy and not reality, he will naturally report his experience by locutions like "I feel *as if* I'm disintegrating." Notice that he does not naturally say "I seem to be dematerializing" or "It seems to me that I'm disintegrating," because these signify that he is under the illusion that he is disintegrating. But, unless he is deranged, this is not the nature of his experience. It does not seem to him that his body is disintegrating; as he would put it, it only "seems *as if*" his body were dematerializing. His experience is not quite like what are called "illusions." When you gaze down the railroad tracks, though you know they run parallel, they nevertheless seem to converge in the distance. They present that illusion. But the peculiar nature of the fantasy-experience is that, though delusion and illusion are both absent, it is appropriately describable by "I feel *as if* . . . ," "It seems *as if* . . . ," or "It is *as if*. . . ." The peculiarity of my fantasy is that I do not believe that I am disintegrating, I do not feel that I am, and it does not seem to me that I am, yet I feel *as if* I am disintegrating.

What is the explanation of this? It is, we suggest, the fact that *feelings are imagined* insofar as they are included within fantasies. In the kind of case we have been discussing, changes in body-image or how I imagine my body are changes in feeling, and when my feelings attach to the way in which I experience changes in my *body-image* rather than to the way I experience changes in my *body,* they are "imagined feelings" that I refer to by "as if" descriptions. The peculiarity of fantasy is the peculiarity of imagined feeling. This is true of other fantasy-experiences, including reading fiction. My feelings of fear, hope, disappointment, etc., are ordinarily "imagined" feelings as I follow the plot from page to page. I have a splendid time moving through the novel though never "really" frightened, hopeful, chagrined, and so on. Experiences under drugs, if not too severe, can resemble reading in this respect. That is, the imagination has been stimulated but without the printed page as stimulus.

Imagination and fantasy are often praised for raising us out of the quotidian rut and revealing what is possible and what is potential. It has been claimed for them that they are superior sources of insight, better than our own eyes and ears for knowing reality as it is; and we can endorse such praise, if more carefully qualified, of fantasy and imagination. However, the description of a fantasy may easily fail to be the description of possible or potential reality. It may be a description of the truly "fantastic," what could never happen. In fantasies we can feel *as if* a round square encloses us, *as if* we are in two places at once, *as if* nothing or everything changes, as if time is unreal, and *as if* one's body is a sort of container. Logic is sufficient to show the impossibility of round squares and thus the unpromising nature of that fantasy, and the facts of life ought to be sufficient to show the unpromising character of the body-as-container fantasy. It looks "fantastic" against the evidence.

Moreover, you might think, because of a certain confusion, that the description of a fantasy *must* be a description, if not of the probable, at least of the possible. You might think that, if you know what it is like to "feel as if" your body were disintegrating, you then know what it is like, at least in some small way, to feel your body disintegrating. You might think that, if you know what it is like to "feel as if" you were outside your body, you then have some hint of what it would be like to be outside your body. But, unless you have felt your body disintegrating or have been outside your body, you have no way of knowing whether "feeling as if" is a clue or hint in the slightest. There is nothing whatever to support the claim that it is. It is perhaps the case that "feeling as if" your body were disintegrating tells you nothing about what it would feel like if your body actually disintegrated. A fantasy may be just a fantasy, not only not the real thing now or ever, but not even a hint of the real thing now or ever.[11]

We take it to be a fact that many people assume that philosophical dualism "supports" what their extraordinary experiences suggest, and that their extraordinary experiences "support" what philosophical dualism suggests. They may even induce such experiences by drugs, autosuggestion, or other means for the purpose of strengthening their belief in dualism. Such people are probably already accustomed to hearing their reasoning characterized as unscientific, illogical, and even inimical to their health. They may agree that, in the scientific sense of the word, their body-image fantasies do not "confirm" the hypothesis of dualism. But they may return to those fantasies, because they delight in the way that those experiences seem to them to "suggest" dualism. They argue that such experiences show dualism to be at least possible and what it would be like to verify it. But this, they may not have heard, is the crucial mistake. For remember: I properly describe my body-image fantasies by "I feel *as if* . . ." and "It seems *as if* . . . ," and these by themselves do not imply anything whatever about what it would feel like if something were actually the case. Evidence beyond the fantasies themselves is required to show whether they are relevant to either the possible or the probable. One can return to fantasies as aesthetic experiences, and one can perhaps use them for creating other aesthetic experiences, as some artists do. But returning to fantasy to learn about reality is being motivated by a big mistake.

8
Memory

1. Biology and Memory

Descartes said, as we noted earlier, that we are always thinking. He could have said, perhaps more justly, that we are always
remembering. For memory enters every present moment, and,
if it did not, the result would be chaotic. Without it, we should
be virtually unable to think, to speak, to recognize, and to
identify anything. If we did not somehow constantly carry with
us a record of the past, we should be unable to make much
sense out of the present.

Some of the most exciting speculations in biology today
concern memory. Martin Wells distinguishes three forms of
memory; the first being short-term memory illustrated by the
telephone number of a stranger that one forgets so quickly after
memorizing it.[1] A second kind is what is called "sensitization,"
also a short-term affair. If you have been accidentally shocked,
say, while repairing an electrical appliance, you may be temporarily "sensitized" to react fearfully to any sudden contact
including nonelectrical ones. The third and most interesting
type of memory is detailed recollection of events that happened
long ago. In animals as well as in humans long-term memory

116

is quite stubborn. "We can anaesthetise animals that we have trained, cool them to temperatures at which all neural activity ceases, disorganize the electrical circuits in their brains, yet none of these treatments eliminates long-term memory traces." [2] Surprisingly little is known about the physiological nature of long-term memory traces. But one suggestive bit of information is that large portions of the brain must be removed to eliminate long-term memory. This indicates that it consists of traces that are numerous and widespread. Another is that long-term memory of an event can be prevented by disrupting the electrical activity of the brain just before the event occurs. Moreover, mental patients receiving electrical shock treatments, for example, do not remember the shock or the events just preceding the shock. Another suggestive fact is that interfering with certain protein synthesis in the brain, by injecting antibiotics like puromycin, blocks the formation of long-term memory.

What is suggested, Wells thinks, is that short-term memory is due to electrical events in the brain. "It is difficult to imagine other forms of storage that could become instantly effective and yet die away completely within a matter of minutes." But long-term memory must have a different basis, something more permanent and structural. One theory is that the electrical traces of short-term memory and sensitization become "growth changes" that are the traces of long-term memory. This is supported by the discovery that nerve cells in the brains of animals that have learned differ from those in untrained animals by containing more RNA (ribonucleic acid), the chemical governing protein synthesis in the nerve cells. The next interesting fact is that, though RNA production increases in any kind of active cell, it is different in those nerve cells exposed to *new* patterns of input, and it is different only so long as the organism is learning. After learning, the RNA molecule reverts to its normal constitution. But, as Wells puts it, "the nervous system is not the same as it was." The changes that occur during learning must apparently consist in the formation of new connections between nerve cells, but its nature is yet to be ascertained.

There is much talk today about the biological hunt for the "memory molecule" or "memory pill." This has been spurred by recent experiments on rats, mice, cats, flatworms, and fish that provoke the claim that memory is transferable from one organism to another. One experimenter claims to have transmitted specific skills from trained to untrained rats by injecting the untrained ones with brain RNA from the trained ones.[3] The properties of RNA are such that it can provide a kind of physiological permanence during the rapid change of chemical compounds in the brain. This does not mean that memory is based upon a single molecular change; indeed, it may rather depend upon the "perpetual ability of millions of different molecules to be manufactured."[4] There is also evidence that learning and memory depend upon increased transmission efficiency in a synapse, the point at which electrical occurrences in one nerve cell influence the activity of the neighboring nerve cell. How this is to be further explained is still a matter of theoretical debate.[5] In any event, experiments with drugs indicate such a conclusion. Drugs like strychnine and Metrazol, by stimulating the central nervous system, apparently cause mice to build short-term into long-term memories. We hear, accordingly, rumors about a future "memory pill." But the present drugs are apparently too dangerous and unpredictable in their effects to constitute any such memory pill. According to Deutsch, "Seekers for a pill to end practice and study forever will have to look elsewhere."[6]

The sense in which we always "remember" is, of course, not that of conscious recall. Our constant memory is in the form of a record of the past somehow stored in our central nervous system, and which, fortunately, serves us happily in its anonymity. Conscious recall of past experiences, while sporadic rather than constant, is no less remarkable. What some researchers stress is the astonishing specificity of detail sometimes present in our recall of the distant past. According to R. W. Gerard, "The problem of recall and its specificity is the real challenge to neurophysiology."[7] The problem is immensely complicated, since recall involves attention, selection of specific details and rejection of others, and symbolization (recollections disguised in symbols). What could be the physiological basis for all this? Gerard speculates that such phenomena of attention and conscious awareness in recall may be due to the influence of the "older and deeper" masses of nerve cells in the upper portion of the brain stem upon the more recently developed neurons of the cerebral cortex. Some evidence of this hypothesis exists, but Gerard, like other researchers, consigns definite answers to those future investigations that everyone expects to occur.

2. Psychology and Memory

Psychology has always studied memory in studying learning, and today its investigations are fused with those of biology, even though, of course, psychologists may refrain from "going under the skin." To be interested in memory is to be interested not only in what makes it succeed but in what makes it fail as well. Concern for memory carries with it a concern for forgetting, for the "interference" that may block one from recalling what one searches for. It is interesting, therefore, to read, according to Ceraso, that "interference continues to be the phenomenon most studied by psychologists interested in memory."[8]

This "interference" theory of forgetting is today more fashionable than the older "decay" theory. The decay theory compares memories to colors that, if not somehow revivified, fade from the "mind's canvas." Forgetting is just memory decaying. Ceraso illustrates the interference theory of forgetting by the professor of ichthyology who, when questioned about his preference for teaching or research, replied that, alas, every time he learned the name of a student he forgot the name of a fish. The point is that learning one thing can interfere with the ability to learn or retain another thing. One theory holds that the interference is not produced by any so-called forgetting process; instead, the interference is a case of mismemory. Things in the past compete for one's present attention, and one forgets some of these because one remembers the "wrong" items. Ceraso, however, thinks that forgetting is not mismemory but is rather the experienced difficulty of picking out the desired or "correct" item from an increasingly large number of things being learned and stored for recall. This might well be true, in view of the fact that the brain is said to be capable of storing something like 10 trillion bits of information in the course of a lifetime.

A. R. Luria's fascinating book *The Mind of a Mnemonist* shows how memory can interest the psychologist in a variety of respects.[9] This book reveals how one mind owning an incredible memory worked. The memory wizard, studied by Luria and others over many years, recollected everything in vivid images. He remembered lists of numbers by associating them with images. He reacted to things synaesthetically, fusing sensations and images of different modalities. He reported that when he was read a Hebrew prayer at the age of three, the words that were not yet understood registered in his mind as puffs of steam or splashes. Whenever he recalled the sounds of those words he "saw" those puffs of steam and splashes. If he heard a certain sound he "saw" a velvet cord pleasantly colored pink-orange.[10] Luria observes that this man's prodigious memory did not depend upon memorizing, and it was not quite what is called "eidetic memory." He found it difficult to distinguish between perceptions and emotions, between images and reality. His was not a "logical" mind, requiring complicated feats of imagery to solve fairly simple problems. His propensity for figurative thinking hampered him in certain tasks; for instance, it was difficult for him to read poetry, because he would lose the poetic meaning of the words in a welter of images. He somehow used imagery to control his pulse rate and body temperature at will. He could apparently "will" the avoidance of pain while the dentist drilled. What most interested Luria was the man's personality. He seemed rather lost in fantasy, alone, seeing life through a haze, as if waiting for something to happen. Luria writes: "Psychology has yet to become a science that is capable of dealing with the really vital aspects of human personality."[11]

He clearly hopes that his study of a man's mind caught up in memories and images may send psychology in the right direction, of dealing with the "really vital aspects" of human personality.

Psychoanalytic theory, of course, has always regarded memory as the key to the vital aspects of personality. Freud believed that self-knowledge, understanding what sort of a person one is and why one is that sort, depends upon recollection of critical events in one's past. He became convinced that the device of free association, of spontaneously uttering whatever comes to mind in association with significant people and events from the past, is superior to hypnosis for true appreciation of recalled occurrences. Freud emphasized the difficulties involved in trying to recall those events that still "bug" us and keep us locked in neurosis. He hypothesized that the effects of events, even of infantile experiences, linger in our *unconscious* and, while hiding there, continue to vex us. As we shut from mind unpleasant prospects like a visit to the dentist, so we *repress* memories of painful experiences like being rejected by one's parents. But repression, according to psychoanalysis, is costly. It produces conflict, guilt, anxiety, and painful confusion. As health depends upon "facing the music" and enduring the sadism of the dentist, so, Freud thought, it also depends upon reliving the hurt of the relevant past experience. Whereas everyone takes for granted the fact that we cannot recall much of our childhood, psychoanalysis asks *why* this is the case.[12] And, according to it, while undoing the process of repression and "facing the past" through recollection is painfully difficult, it is ultimately rewarding if successful. It produces "abreaction," an emotional discharge that follows the active recall of those experiences that one has desperately sought to shut from mind. This emotional discharge can be compared to the "release" felt when the aching tooth is at last removed. We can see, then, not only how psychoanalytic theory conceives the relation between self-knowledge and memory but also how it explains in its own way the dynamics of forgetting.[13] Psychoanalytic theory is throughout controversial, but it wins considerable critical acceptance in its insistence upon the influence of our remote past on our present attitudes and in its insistence in the interest of mental health upon our need, often through memory, to understand that remote past.

Psychology, it appears, finds the phenomena of remembering and forgetting to be significant everywhere. For example, a connection between memory (or forgetting) and obesity has now been announced. It is reported that fat people, who have lost much weight during a dieting period, fail to register that salutary fact in their images of themselves. They continue to "see" themselves as they were prior to dieting. Tests seem to show that, with astonishing uniformity, dieters cannot assimilate their recent loss of weight into their body-images, and these same people almost always eat their return to their original obese condition. The odd fact, the explanation of which is still in doubt, is that these people seem unable to forget how they looked when obese and unable to remember how they more recently looked while dieting. That the abilities to forget and to remember are involved is indicated by testing the time-sense of these dieters. They were asked to estimate the length of a series of recorded sounds, to decide whether they were longer or shorter than one second. Oddly, while dieting they concluded that the sounds were longer than they actually were, but while in their usual obese state they made more accurate conclusions. One hypothesis being considered is that the apparent alteration of time-sense during dieting is biochemically based, connected perhaps with the shrinkage of fat cells (though their numbers remain constant) when losing weight. On this hypothesis, there is perhaps some hidden link between memory and a dieter's wanting to nourish his fat cells to their original fullness.[14]

3. Philosophy and Memory

Philosophers sometimes ask questions like "Is (at this moment) the future real?" and "Is (at this moment) the past real?" They sometimes mean by these, "Does (at this moment) the future exist?" and "Does (at this moment) the past exist?"

A philosopher might argue, for instance, that memory shows that past events continue in existence, that the past in being recalled becomes "present to" one's consciousness.[15]

Most philosophers, however, join common sense in regarding a memory-experience as the present recall of events that are past and therefore not present. They emphasize, in this connection, that there is always a "delusive" element in memory.[16] The past is never exactly reproduced in recollection. It is recalled selectively, parts of it always edited out. In fact, a remembered event rarely even seems to be present; we are seldom deluded into thinking that the past has literally risen Lazaruslike again. Some philosophers have said that the memory-image of something is fainter or less vivid than the original perception of it, and others have noted that the peculiar "feel" of a memory-experience is one of being "detached" from the past event even while recalling it. One feels very much in the present no matter how vivid the memory.[17] Philosophers have also recently emphasized that images are unnecessary for much of what we call memory, and, accordingly, there is no temptation to absorb the remembered into the present remembering. In remembering the alphabet, my name, where I live, and how to skate, I need no special imagery. To say that I remember something often means simply that I have not forgotten something previously learned.[18]

Philosophers also ask whether it is possible to check a memory without using memory. Can you verify your claim to remember something independent of other and fallible claims to remember? It seems apparent, despite ingenious arguments to the contrary, that it is not possible. For instance, suppose you check your claim to remember that you parked your car on Broadway. You find your car there, but this in itself only shows that you were right in *believing* that it is there but not necessarily that you were right in claiming to *remember* where it is. Unless you remember other things connected with the occasion of parking your car, you lack evidence that your success in locating it is really due to memory. In any event, when you locate your car, you must of course *remember* that *it* is your car, and this memory-claim necessarily figures in defending your original claim to remember the car's location. It takes a memory, along with other evidence, to check a memory.[19]

4. Memory and Retrospection

Philosophers have often thought that knowing oneself involves knowing one's mental and bodily states as they succeed one another, and that this requires introspection. But philosophers have also concluded that, as it is often conceived, introspection cannot or does not exist. They have argued that one difficulty is as follows: Suppose you have a pain; to have a pain is to be aware of it; then, to introspect that means that you must be aware of being aware that you have the pain. But, they claim, you never find that, besides the pain, you are also aware of something called the awareness of the pain. If you insisted that you did make such a finding, they would ask if you can be aware of being aware of being aware of the pain. How many awarenesses can you simultaneously be aware of? Also, does not the very queerness of this question show that it is initially absurd to talk about "being aware of being aware?" Further, how can you really introspect the awareness of the pain, if this means that you must simultaneously attend both to the pain and to your awareness of it? Still further, how can you introspect a state like intense anger without "cooling" it or modifying it? Introspecting it would not seem to give you an accurate "inner" look at the anger but would rather seem to *change* the state that you are trying to observe. Finally, our states succeed each other so quickly that we can only "observe" them at best *after* their occurrence. That is, we can only *retrospect* them; we cannot really catch them as they occur. For these reasons, some philosophers have concluded that the only kind of introspection that occurs is retrospection.[20]

Retrospection may or may not involve memory, depending upon how recent or how remote is the recollected event. William James and A. J. Ayer, among others, have maintained that you can be directly aware now of something that occurred a second ago, that it is still "given" to your present awareness. You are still witnessing it, and it would be a mistake to say that you remember it.[21] When you listen to a melody, you hear several notes *simultaneously* even though they happen successively, and it would be a mistake to suppose that the succession of each note by the next is registered by a separate act of remembering. That one thing happens before or after another is revealed to you *now*, as directly and as immediately as the fact that one thing is above or below another is revealed to you now. You would never say that you remembered that the one occurred before the other, if that happened but a second or two ago. To say that you remembered it implies more remoteness in the past. Hence, despite the paradoxical sound of it, the past is sometimes noted in the present and is not always something remembered. When you retrospect your own states, therefore, memory is only involved when they are sufficiently remote in time.

The primary function of memory is to keep a record of the past, as it is also of retrospection of the "immediate past" that does not involve memory. Noting retrospectively that you just felt jealous, just saw a flash, just smelled powder, etc., is important for keeping a record of your experience. Retrospection, however, may be more than just keeping a record. As we shall emphasize below, it may be a *review* of the record that includes diagnoses, interpretations, and speculations about one's past. But another though largely unacknowledged fact, which we want to pause upon here, is that retrospection can even *reveal* previously unnoticed parts of the past.

Can you remember something of which you were in no way aware at the time it occurred? Appealing to the fact that we *mean* by "what is remembered" what we were once aware of before, you properly answer in the negative. It makes no sense to speak of remembering what you were never aware of. It is possible, however, to remember what you do not remember being aware of. You might recall a face in the crowd, for instance, but be unable to recollect the experience of being aware that you saw the face when you did. The face but not the occasion of seeing it returns in memory. Thus, though you cannot remember what you were not previously aware of, you can vividly remember what you do not remember being aware of. It may be that you have forgotten the occasion of being aware of it, or it may be that you were "unconsciously aware" of the face when seen.

But suppose you have *this* kind of experience: You seem to notice something, while remembering a certain slice of the past, that seems not to be noticed again but rather seems to be noticed *for the first time.* Are you entitled to think that you *are* now aware *for the first time* of something in the past? Is it even possible? We might try to explain this experience of seeming to be aware for the first time of a past something (a face in a crowd) by saying that you consciously saw it but have forgotten the occasion of seeing it or that you "unconsciously saw" it and are now remembering what you were unconsciously aware of. Our explanation, requiring that you were previously aware of the face in the crowd, denies that you can be aware of it for the first time while remembering a slice of the past. But this explanation is in fact unjustified. Given that "being aware again" is what is *meant* by "remembering," all we can conclude is that you *cannot remember* that of which you are aware for the first time. We are not entitled to conclude that you cannot be aware now and for the first time of something in the past that is not even remembered. We agree that, when genuinely remembering, you "see," "hear," "taste," "smell," "feel," things from the past (the quotes around these words signifying the mode of awareness to be explained below). We are not empowered to conclude that you cannot "see," "hear," "taste," "smell," "feel" unremembered things during what is essentially a memory-experience.

Suppose you are remembering the crowd in the park yesterday. As you allow the details of the recollected scene to unfold, you suddenly "see" a certain face. It seems to you that you never saw it before, a face you are certain that you do not recall having been aware of before. Suppose, further, that no evidence appears that you had been "unconsciously aware" of the face yesterday; that is, there is no evidence that your present behavior and attitude are influenced by unconscious awareness of it. Finally, independent evidence shows that the same face *was* in the crowd yesterday. You are surely warranted in thinking, however baffling the explanation for it, that you are now "seeing" a face as it was in the past but not one that you remember by virtue of having been aware of it before.

Is there an explanation that makes sense of your claim to "see" something unremembered in the experience of remembering something else? The most likely one is that a *memory-experience* can re-create complexes or mosaics from the past. Memory-experience re-creates whole experiences, details of which may have totally escaped awareness when they occurred. Memory-experience can bring back most of a past scene, including details not remembered because not even unconsciously noticed before. Because there were so many faces in the crowd, it is only natural that you were not aware of all that you stared at. But *memory-experience* returns the scene so well that, when inspected *now,* you become aware of the *unremembered* as well as the remembered details included in it. Memory-experience is remarkable in giving you a second and third "look" at a past episode such that you "see," "hear," etc., some of its details *for the first time.* The explanation notes that a memory-experience can include more than remembering, and, if it is asked *how* this can happen, the answer may be—that is how the brain works.

Philosophers have pondered how to characterize memory-consciousness indicated by "see," "hear," etc. Recollecting is an experience in which one "sees" the past; it is not, for instance, merely inferring that something happened. Whether one is genuinely remembering what one "sees" or whether (given the preceding discussion) one is "seeing" it for the first time, the experience is somehow analogous to perceiving something.[22] But we cannot say that we are really seeing anything. We are not seeing the past again, for to say that would imply that the past has reappeared for present perception. In closing my eyes and "seeing" yesterday's game I'm not really seeing anything.

Nor does it help to say that I "seem to see" the past, because that suggests that I might be under the illusion that the past is perceptually present. In recalling yesterday's game, however, I do not "seem to see" it as I "seem to see" a pool of water that is in fact a mirage. Finally, it does not help to say that I either see or seem to see images. We often *have* images in memory-experience, but they are not things that we see or seem to see. We see images of ourselves in mirrors and lakes; we can observe them and can watch them move as we move. But the image I have of myself in recalling yesterday's game is not something I can observe; it does not move with me.[23] How do you know that you are having an image? Not by more closely looking at something, not by more closely noticing anything.

To have a memory-image is to have an experience that somewhat resembles an experience wherein one sees or seems to see something. We can express the resemblance by saying that it is "as if" I see yesterday's game in remembering it. The "as if" locution is valuable, since it indicates both the resemblance and the lack of it of a memory-experience to a perceptual experience. The locution indicates the special character, what some philosophers have called the peculiar "feel," of memory-experience. The peculiar nature of a remembering is that it is "as if" I see or seem to see something in the past, though I do not want to describe it as a seeing or seeming to see, since it is quite different from such. One need only consult one's own experience to verify this. The "feel" of a memory experience, insofar as it is a "feel" of "seeing" a past something, is expressible in the "as if" vocabulary. It is not that I see or seem to see it, but it is indeed "as if" I see or seem to see it. Perhaps this says about all that can be said about the "seeing" of memory.

5. Memory and Self

It is perhaps true that "seeing" something from the past *for the first time* is a rare phenomenon in memory, and, to that extent, its significance is indeed limited. But neither should its importance be slighted. It makes us note that remembering can be more than routine, that we may be able to retain a record of a past to which we were exposed but of which we were unaware. In some cases, that may be significant for self-knowledge; in those possibly rare instances, coming to know such details from the past may affect certain judgments that we place upon ourselves. It shows the precariousness of arguing, if I now "see" a past something of which I was consciously unaware when it occurred, that I *must* have been "unconsciously" aware of it. It further shows how remembering can be exploratory and voluntary, how we can deliberately engage in "re-seeing" our past but with some surprises possible. It helps us to appreciate that memory is not always a checking of the record only. Memory is not always a passive recall of a past experience, nor is it always a search for a specific something to fill in a gap. The paradigm of memory is not that of trying to recollect a forgotten name that is on the tip of one's tongue. Also, retrospection is not always an attending to what is "just past" in order to keep the record straight. Retrospection is often a roaming reinterpretation of one's whole life. Retrospecting is often reinterpreting, while reviewing one's life, what one was in the light of the present, what one is in the light of the past.

What should the philosophy of psychology emphasize about retrospecting that is deliberate and exploratory? First, that it is essential to keeping a record of the continuity of one's past; it prevents the kind of passive recall responsible for the mere repetition in memory of only a few special experiences, while forgetting all the others. In deliberately exploring one's past experiences through recall, one keeps alive much of one's past that otherwise dies through neglect. Secondly, that memory is essentially *egoistic*. In remembering it is generally *oneself* that is in the center of the picture. I remember what *I* did, what *I* saw, what *I* experienced. Running through one's memories is somewhat like looking at old movies in which oneself is the star. This is important for understanding how memory is related to self-knowledge.

Knowing who I am, where I live, etc., obviously depends upon an intact memory. But knowing who I am in more subtle respects (like understanding my motivations in certain situations, like knowing how others really see me, knowing the strengths and weaknesses of character that are typically mine, etc.) requires more than intact memory. Among other things, it requires a remembering that deliberately probes the past. Psychoanalytic theory emphasizes the need to recall traumatic experiences and to understand them as it understands them. Self-knowledge, however, is not confined to knowing the nature of one's neuroses. A fuller knowledge of self cannot be tied to the recall of a few critical events; it demands a more exploratory and far-ranging memory. The kind of memory that we are emphasizing here is the voluntary and exploratory remembering that is due to *self-interest.* This is not the same as an automatically good memory, for a person may recollect an amazing amount of his past but indifferently. He may live in the past but care little for it. We are not in fact extolling the sort of remembering that is colloquially referred to as "living in the past." We are not speaking, for instance, of the memories in which some elderly people happily resign their lives. Nor are we speaking of memories that please and enhance self-esteem, for these may be largely irrelevant to self-knowledge.

The point is that self-knowledge, in its more subtle and interesting aspects, is a function of self-interest. We risk the generalization that people who do not voluntarily probe the past have little self-interest, that deliberate, exploratory memory is a measure of one's cognitive concern for self. When memory is called to assist the cause of self-knowledge, we do not recall just to recall. We use the memories as data for reinspecting our past selves in terms of what we know and are now, for reinterpreting our present selves in terms of what we knew and were then. You may have wept when your father died, and you may in recall have thought that you did so out of weakness, and now, when your daughter dies, you think yourself strong in remaining dry-eyed. But, in the light of other considerations, including a recall of the past, you may be led to revise these judgments. In any event, how much knowledge you have of yourself and how much interest you take in yourself are indicated by how much of your time you give to this kind of recall.

9

Introspection

1. Concepts of Introspection

Ordinary language is peculiar in including the adjective "introspective" but excluding the noun "introspection" and the verb "introspect." You rarely hear the noun and verb in colloquial talk. You rarely hear, for instance, someone asking, "What are you introspecting?" or someone reporting, "I'm introspecting such-and-such." But you do hear someone occasionally characterize a person as "introspective," and what is meant is that the person so described is introverted, self-involved, withdrawn. Ordinary opinion says that being introspective is dangerous; it causes you to lose contact with reality and to suffer the consequences of extravagant self-consciousness. Philosophers have supported ordinary opinion on the point. Immanuel Kant (1724–1804) cautioned against keeping a diary of your thoughts and attitudes, because it might cause you, through the loss of perspective that results from self-preoccupation, to go literally mad. Introspective individuals are advised to divorce their thoughts from themselves.

Nevertheless, many psychologists and philosophers have defended introspection as an indispensable source of knowledge.

131

Unlike the ordinary man, they do ask "What are you intro-specting?" and, unlike ordinary opinion, they. do not equate "introspective" with "introverted." Their claims for introspec-tion are obviously not endorsements of morbid self-preoccupa-tion. They consider introspection to be what William James called it, "looking into our minds and reporting what we there discover."[1] On this view, introspecting is paying attention to internal states. It is fixing attention upon states of consciousness that would otherwise go virtually unnoticed or unappreciated. It affords more exact apprehension of one's own psychological states.

Kant objected to this concept of introspection, arguing that fixing attention upon a subjective state necessarily disturbs that state; and what one introspectively reports is therefore a dis-torted version of what one set out to observe. Two kinds of replies have been made to this. Wilhelm Wundt (1832–1920) and E. B. Titchener (1867–1927) argued that Kant assumed introspection to be necessarily a conscious process, i.e., self-consciously engaged in. He supposed, according to them, that the inevitable concern with the fact that one is introspecting a subjective state will alter the state or will prevent clear apprehension of it. Wundt disagreed: "In his attention to the phenomena under observation, the observer in psychology, no less than the observer in physics, completely forgets to give subjective attention to the state of observing."[2] That is, one can introspect without being conscious (and therefore distracted by it) of doing so. The second reply accuses Kant's argument of being self-contradictory. How could Kant know, except on the basis of introspection, that introspection does alter the state being introspected?[3] He certainly could not have learned this by *not* paying attention to his inner states!

The classical concept of introspection is associated with Wundt. The proper business of psychology, he believed, is to study states of consciousness. These turn out to be complexes capable of analysis into more elementary ingredients. Using chemistry as his model, he conceived of subjective states like attitudes, perceptions, and ideas as molecules that are constituted out of atoms like sensations, feelings, and images. The task for introspection is to analyze complex states of mind, which may not at first appear to be sensory, into their sensory elements. Scientific introspection differs from casual, everyday introspection in being analytical, in resolving psychological molecules into their constituent psychological atoms.

Several facts contributed to the decline of interest in classical introspection. Many psychologists questioned the importance of the results obtained by it. Others were discouraged by the fact that even trained introspectionists often could not agree in their analyses. The Würzburg school threw suspicion upon the Wundt–Titchener concept of introspection in claiming to have discovered, through introspection, that states of mind exist that are not analyzable into sensory elements. In the face of animal psychology, behaviorism, and Gestalt psychology, classical introspection virtually disappeared from professional psychology.[4]

Whether introspection is fallible or infallible has always been debated. Franz Brentano in 1874 wrote: "The phenomena inwardly apprehended are true in themselves. As they appear . . . so they are in reality. Who then can deny that in this a great superiority of psychology over the physical sciences comes to light?" To this William James replied: "If to *have* feelings or thoughts in their immediacy were enough, babies in the cradle would be psychologists, and infallible ones."[5] James emphasized the difficulties involved in adequately introspecting our states of consciousness, and others agreed with him that introspection is really *retrospection*. After all, introspection is a process that takes time. When we attempt an accurate description of a complex state of mind, it may require a twenty-minute account, thus proving that we are really recollecting, a process that is surely fallible. The view that introspection is actually a form of retrospection meets the objection that states of consciousness cannot be introspected because they succeed each other too rapidly to permit being attended to as they occur. We cheerfully concede that introspection is not a source of *infallible* knowledge about one's subjective states.

Gestalt psychology complicated discussions of introspection. Max Wertheimer noted in 1912 that you can seem to see something move even though there is no moving stimulus object. The phenomenon of perceived movement in the absence of physical movement is thus a conscious rather than a physical occurrence. Classical or Wundtian introspection requires the analysis of this into sensory elements like images and sensations. But, Wertheimer argued, this phenomenon (like others such as closure and object-constancy emphasized by Gestalt psychology) is interesting in itself. What is needed is not a dissection of it into something else but rather a more careful description of its character and of the conditions under which it occurs. Describing the *phenomenon* as faithfully as possible, instead of trying to analyze it "chemically," became known as *phenomenological* description. Phenomenological reporting was more fashionable than classical introspection by 1930.[6] It was also called "introspection." But, because it refers to how the *physical* environment *appears* under certain conditions, phenomenological introspection is in fact an instance of perceptual reporting. Phenomenological introspecting is noting how things perceptually appear, even if deceptively. Some thinkers considered this confusing, on the grounds that "introspection" was originally introduced to distinguish a kind of awareness that is "internal" rather than "external," a kind of awareness not to be confused with observing how the external world looks or seems to look. Some proposed calling phenomenological reports like those of Wertheimer "inspection," reserving "introspection" for the attention paid, not to the external world, but to the *inner* world of thoughts and feelings. Whether such a distinction can be upheld is still a matter of debate; some arguing, to the contrary, that any attempt to distinguish sharply between introspection and perceptual observation (including phenomenological reporting) is necessarily artificial.[7]

How do you discover your motives? Your intentions? Your hopes? Your beliefs? Your fears and affections? How do you come to know these vital and intimate features of yourself? It

used to be said, in reply, "by introspection," by looking into
your own mind and reporting what is discovered there. But
this answer has been severely criticized by twentieth-century
philosophy and psychology. It is now agreed that self-knowledge is too strenuous an enterprise to be achieved simply by
looking into one's mind. Behavioral psychologists and Freudian
psychoanalysts seem united on this point. The behaviorists say
that the test of what one wants, believes, loves, hopes for, etc.,
is always how one behaves. You may in all sincerity assert that
you want peace, that you believe that the philosophical life
is superior to the political, that you love your parents, and that
you hope to overcome an addiction. But behaviorists and
Freudians have dignified a suspicion of common sense into a
contemporary slogan: Your sincere testimony about yourself
always runs the risk of self-deception, and in the end you find
out about yourself as you do about others, not by resting on
self-testimony but by looking to the sorts of things that you
do and experience. Among the reminders that twentieth-century man keeps in the forefront of his consciousness is the
constant possibility of self-deception.

The point emphasized by both behaviorists and Freudians
is that knowledge of one's motives, beliefs, etc., requires complicated *diagnosis*. One cannot determine such things about oneself
just by introspecting in the way that one may do to check if
the headache is still there, if the pain is still in the same part
of the abdomen, if the anticipation of tomorrow's trip pleases,
and so on. But it must be admitted that behavioral psychology
and psychoanalysis begin to diverge when the conditions of an
adequate diagnosis are defined. Experimental psychology that
is behavioristically oriented finds the test of what you want,
believe, etc., in how you *overtly behave,* in your public performances that can be studied by sophisticated observers. You may
believe, for instance, that you are prepared to be a good pilot,
artist, or parent; but behavioral psychology regards this as but
a claim to be tested by how you actually perform under pre-
scribed conditions. Any introspecting that you do is a claim.
It cannot be its own test. Psychoanalysis, however, holds that

it is necessary to consult what one *experiences,* in addition to how one publicly behaves, to learn what are the "deep" wants and beliefs of a person. How one *feels* in certain situations, what one *dreams* on a given night, and what one *says to oneself* on a certain occasion, are examples of factors beyond overt behavior that psychoanalysis insists upon as relevant to the diagnosis of what one wants, believes, hopes, etc. Psychoanalysis and clinical psychology join behaviorists in distrusting overly-simple concepts of introspection, but they part company in retaining the concept of introspection as a process of self-questioning, self-dialogue, *self-analysis.* To illustrate this, we turn to two recent and interesting introspective investigations.

2. *Two Recent Introspective Studies*

The first to be reviewed here is by David Bakan.[8] He conducted a self-experiment, designed to show the utility of introspective analysis as a scientific tool despite behavioristic objections, to discover what is involved in a person's retaining and revealing secrets. Bakan calls it a "miniature" experiment, because it lasted but five days for about one and one-half hours each day. He hit upon the retention and revelation of secrets, since a person's way of doing such is not typically connected with a specific pattern of overt behavior. It seems a topic inherently amenable to introspective investigation. The procedure was very simple. Bakan wrote at a typewriter whatever entered his mind, in the attitude that what he wrote would never be made public. On one occasion he recalled a conversation with a fellow academician who had emphasized his own conscientiousness. Bakan asked on his typewriter why his acquaintance had protested being conscientious, then found himself typing next that he (Bakan) realized he himself felt guilty about a lack of conscientiousness. This was his own "secret," he typed, noting simultaneously that he had not been able to reveal this to himself until he had remembered a conversation that, so to speak, allowed him not to endure his guilt alone. So he remembered a conversation with a friend suffering from a similar guilt, a similar secret. The psychological fact learned here, Bakan then observed to himself, is that we are more apt to reveal a secret guilt on the occasion when we think it is shared. This was the first proposition learned from his miniature study.

Others subsequently emerging were these: A person with a secret guilt will tend to set up occasions where he can recognize that others share it. Also, we tend to retain our secrets to avoid negative responses from others and to retain their favorable impression of us. People sharing a secret will create a special, "in-group" language for discussing it. We are prone to be secretive about our intellectual limitations. We often conceal a secret by pretending to reveal something, or, if actually revealing it we may try to cover it up under the guise that we are only telling a joke. A person whose secret is his constant depression will tend to assert the opposite, that he is generally happy. We reprehend ourselves in revealing secrets to others to forestall reprehensions from them. We tend to betray the secrets of one group when we leave that group for another, and, if a secret-sharer betrays us, we betray him.

Bakan makes several observations about the above information and the experiment yielding it. He emphasizes the importance of the psychology of secrets. What a person values, what he holds for himself as goals, and what he identifies himself with, are all possibly secret even to himself. Knowing the dynamics of retaining and revealing secrets is obviously relevant to assisting such a person to self-illumination. The value of a psychology of secrets is not confined to showing an individual facts about himself; it clearly extends to problems of economics, marriage, politics, military strategy, and so on. In short, what one learns through an introspective study need not relate uniquely to oneself but can often be generalized and tested appropriately. The value of the introspective experiment resides both in revealing truths about oneself and in suggesting hypotheses that apply to others as well.

Bakan is fully aware of a possible demurrer to the foregoing. You may say that the so-called "information" yielded by his introspecting at his typewriter is really rather obvious. Live a little, and you quickly learn such facts about secrets, and the recourse to introspection is seen to be superfluous. The "information" Bakan gets from his miniature study is not really "news." Or if it is, it can be more effectively obtained from studies of a person's relations (in behavior) to others than from a person's relation (introspective) to himself. Bakan makes two points in reply. First, you do not more effectively obtain such information about yourself (and possibly others) through other techniques. The value of the introspective technique is in its "directness," minimizing the possibility of error. Since introspection here is admittedly retrospection, the method depends upon memory and is thus fallible. But various sources of error are avoided. There is no problem of the subject failing to cooperate, of trying to fool the investigator, of failing to grasp instructions, of refusing to believe in the investigator's expressed intentions, of refusing to be candid because of another's presence, and so on. Secondly, the value of propositions learned through the "miniature" experiment is precisely in their obviousness, in their tendency to elicit an "of course" response because they are self-evident. But Bakan does not really explain why the obviousness of introspectively learned propositions is so meritorious, a fact he himself seems to realize in suggesting that the "self-evidential" nature of such propositions is a concept perhaps requiring philosophical clarification. Maybe the point is that the truth of propositions about oneself (and possibly others) emerging from an introspective study like Bakan's really "sink in," "register," "hit the nail on the head," "come home to one." Their truth is *appreciated* and not merely vaguely known. When they come to mind, such propositions elicit the response "How true!" and "How deeply true!" This does indeed seem to be an important psychological fact about propositions emerging from an introspective study.

It should be noticed that what Bakan means by "introspection" is considerably more complicated than any process of "looking into one's mind" to see if the prospect, say, of tomorrow's trip still pleases. Bakan's little experiment involved an oscillation between allowing his mind to fill up freely with memories, associations, thoughts, images, etc., and placing upon those mental contents an "analysis" that they themselves suggest, though in the light of what one knows through experience and theory. This is an essential pattern of introspection that is self-diagnosis or self-interpretation, and it characterizes our second example of recent introspective studies, an investigation into dreams and fantasies by Jerome Singer.[9]

Singer observes that "as an introspective individual, I hope I can stimulate a more effective attack on the many research problems having to do with daydreaming and conscious fantasy."[10] It is not the purpose of introspection, he states, to make conclusive statements about phenomena nor to test hypotheses definitively; instead, its function is to show what is important to a person by discovering the nature of his dreams (night and day) and fantasies. This then sets guidelines for the experimental researcher as to what is *relevant* in the way of tests and hypotheses for understanding the person in terms of personality theory. An important source of information about what matters to people, indicating the "vital" aspects of their personalities, is daydreams. Singer found that his daydreams fell into two categories, the first being recurrent and elaborate ones from childhood and the second being streams of associations and interior monologues. Those recurring from childhood were of the "central figure" variety. The central figure in these fantasies was a football hero, a great statesman, and a distinguished composer. Living in daydreams focusing upon an "heroic" figure indicates a high degree of achievement motivation, a fact confirmed by Singer's actual behavioral patterns. And although he never became a football hero, statesman, or composer, he did engage in activities associated with each career. He eventually abandoned the study of music, he thinks, largely because his own musical efforts seemed so inferior to his fantasy. Clinical research confirms this, since it is often the case that people cease creative work, because they are victimized by an extravagant fantasy standard that makes their every effort seem inadequate.

Singer notes that the emotions accompanying the "central figure" fantasies were usually pleasant and mildly exciting. Fantasies are generally less exciting or joyous than actual achievement; nevertheless, they usually yield a considerable degree of excitement and pleasure. Sometimes an unpleasant feeling of shame accompanied the childhood fantasies, undoubtedly due to his knowing that he would be called "childish" if discovered enjoying them. But this did not present a serious problem, since he had learned to internalize them for private use only and was not disposed, as are some people, to view one's own fantasies suspiciously. Another element in his recurrent fantasies, besides achievement motivation and narcissism, was the impulse to make stories out of them. Each fantasy was elaborated by him into a tale. He had done this since early childhood, indicating that what Freud called "secondary process thinking" had occurred early in his fantasy life. That is, he had imposed upon his fantasies a logical structure and organization that go into the composing of a narrative. Turning fantasies into stories is significant, because it serves to distinguish fantasy and reality. For example, Singer did not confuse himself with the heroes of his daydreams, even though partial identification with them might occur. His enjoyment of his daydreams did not blur his sense of reality, no matter how vivid the imagery. He used daydreaming to fill time or to escape a boring occasion, and he concludes that an extensive fantasy life may reinforce rather than weaken one's sense of how fantasy and reality differ. He also suggests that constant acquaintance with one's daydream world makes it sufficiently familiar that it does not appear menacing, provoking anxious responses. People unaccustomed to daydreaming may find sudden fantasies, a certain image, a special sexual idea, a death wish, a certain desire, etc., so shocking that anxiety results. They may even fear that they are hallucinating. Singer believes that his introspections show a direct relation between fantasy and overt behavior, and that those theorists are mistaken who assume that what you do in fantasy you will not do in reality. Studies besides Singer's indicate that there is a tendency to express overtly, at least in some degree, what occurs in one's daydreams.[11]

The second class of reverie-type activity is more often encountered, Singer says of his own experience, than the recurrent, elaborate daydreams carried on from childhood. It includes minor "cognitive footnotes" to perception, like the internal expression of "curiosity about a lone distant light." It includes a running internal comment or interpretation of what one is perceiving or experiencing. This may take the form of an "associative image," as exemplified in Proust's "Madeleine crumb which revives by its taste a sudden flood of memories unfolding like Japanese paper flowers in a bowl of water."[12] Or it may take the form of interior monologue; this is less common, Singer says, than associative imagery and develops later psychologically. It is to some extent a function of literary sophistication. Singer's introspecting revealed a connection between his interior *verbal* monologues and defensive behavior. He recalled that, as a shy adolescent, he might remain aloof at a dance, and, while looking serenely detached from the whole scene, he would conduct a silent verbal monologue that invariably upgraded himself and downgraded those in full frolic.

Singer's introspective or retrospective study of night dreaming shows that dreams at night are essentially like daydreams. He found that he could fall asleep quickly and almost always awaken with the memory of a dream. He used an alarm clock to check this, at intervals ranging from three minutes to one hour. There seemed to be no relation between the interval of sleep and the clarity of the recollected dream. The dreams usually centered upon personal and unresolved problems, and, interestingly enough, there is generally no continuity of dream content with the events or experiences occurring just before going to sleep. Another interesting disclosure is that vivid dreaming occurred within seconds of falling asleep. The content of dreams tended to be less detailed after short rather than long intervals of sleep, although reasonably detailed dreams can occur within a five-minute nap.

Among Singer's many interesting findings in his book *Day-dreaming* is a sociological one. There are substantial differences in daydreaming between different ethnic groups. Daydream frequencies are highest among Italians, Jews, and Negroes, and are lowest among Anglo-Saxons. Recent immigrants daydream more than do those established in the United States. The daydreams of Negroes are concrete and realistic, those of Jews and Anglo-Saxons less so. The Irish excel in daydreams that are mystical and fantastical. Jews, Negroes, and Italians are given to erotic daydreaming. It is perhaps the case that assimilation into Anglo-Saxon Protestant culture tends to diminish the extent of fantasy-experience. In any case, when everything is considered, Singer takes a view different from Freud's about daydreams, reveries, and fantasies. Believing that all fantasy springs from repressed desires, Freud said, "Happy people never make fantasies, only unsatisfied ones do." [13] To the contrary, says Singer; his introspective, clinical, and sociological studies rather show that persons who are willing to "fantasize" are persons willing to see themselves in perspective, willing to engage in imaginative living, and willing to have fun in doing so. [14]

3. Introspection and Philosophy

These studies of Bakan and Singer will prove useful in appraising the attitude of contemporary philosophy toward introspection. The comments made today by Anglo-Saxon "analytic" philosophy about introspection are mostly negative. Due largely to the influence of Ludwig Wittgenstein and Gilbert Ryle, contemporary philosophy emphasizes that philosophical problems arise out of conceptual confusions, and that, accordingly, the proper business of philosophy is the analysis and clarification of concepts. It is commonly said that introspection is irrelevant to this task, a fact that one must particularly appreciate when analyzing psychological concepts. Secondly, philosophers have been impressed by the decline of introspection as a method of investigation in laboratory psychology. They have more or less joined the behaviorists in denying the relevance of introspection for self-knowledge, arguing that we really find out about ourselves in the ways that we make discoveries about others.[15]

Wittgenstein repeatedly warned against trying to understand a psychological concept through introspecting. He showed how you might be tempted to try to explain the concept of sensation to yourself by "looking into your mind" and scrutinizing your present sensations. But you cannot explain the concept of a sensation by describing sensations. You explicate a concept, he urged, in showing the varieties of contexts in which the words expressing it are used. Suppose you are silently presenting to yourself a series of Russian words. Can you, just by introspecting the experience, decide whether you are *thinking* or not? Will introspecting the experience tell you what the concept of thinking is? No, because you must know the relevant things about the *context* in which your experience of silently saying the Russian words occurs. If the context includes such facts as that you do not understand Russian, that you are only babbling to yourself some Russian words once heard, that you had done this deliberately in order not to think and to relax your mind, then you would deny that your experience is a thinking one. The point is that you need to know more (the nature of the context) than merely what you can introspect to know whether the concept of thinking applies to the particular experience. Wittgenstein expressed it graphically: "If God had looked into our minds, he would not have been able to see there what we were speaking of." [16] God would also need to know, beyond the contents of our minds or our present experiences, the context in which they occur to know whether and what we were thinking. There are other equally important arguments that establish the impossibility of learning or employing concepts through introspection.

But from the fact that psychological concepts cannot be explained introspectively, it does not follow, as some philosophers intimate, that introspection is always irrelevant. (After all, God may not know whether I am thinking merely by looking into my mind, but He will also not know it by *not* looking into my mind.) The point is that, all things being equal, we would usually conclude that a person who is introspectively sensitive to sensation, thoughts, and feelings, has a better grasp, in some respects, of the concepts of sensation, thought, and feeling than a person who is introspectively insensitive. A person whose introspections prepare him to agree or disagree with Aristotle that images are indispensable for thinking is a person prepared to answer certain questions about the concept of thinking; to that extent, he has a better grasp of the concept than one not so prepared. It seems impossible to exclude introspection from the activity, taken broadly, of clarifying various psychological concepts. The concept of introspection itself needs more careful discussion by philosophers. It is reasonable to suppose that, in some respects, introspectively sensitive thinkers will throw special light on the concept. Citing the studies of Bakan and Singer had the purpose of conveying this point in some detail.

The development of contemporary "analytic" philosophy is a direct result of the recent separation of philosophy and psychology as distinct professional disciplines. The philosopher is now forbidden "to do" psychology (especially of an introspective sort), and he takes his job to be instead the "analysis" of concepts. It is often contended nowadays that former philosophers and psychologists went wrong just at those points where they ran philosophical and psychological questions together. Hume is sometimes criticized for having tried to introspect the referent of the first-person pronoun. Locke is criticized wherever he seemed to appeal to introspection in defending his view that some ideas are abstract, and Berkeley is similarly rebuked in arguing the opposed view that all ideas are imagelike. Further, introspection is said to be irrelevant to the question whether mental as well as physical "acts" occur; irrelevant also to the question whether judgments are made but neither in words nor images.

C. A. Mace, for example, has argued that what we thought to be problems solvable by introspection are really to be settled through analysis of the concepts involved.[17] Mace believes that introspective disputes relevant to philosophy are curious indeed. It is very odd that introspective reports conflict as to whether abstract ideas, images, mental acts, the awareness of awareness, etc., ever or commonly occur. According to Mace, "These endeavours have been in the main ineffective, because misdirected. The facts are there for everyone to 'see,' but we do not know how to *say* what we 'see.'"[18] That is, the introspective facts are plain enough for everyone to "see," so hesitations and conflicts in introspective reporting must result from the fact that we do not know how to describe what we "introspectively see." In other words, we do not know the relevant concepts required for an adequate description. What is needed, therefore, is an *analysis* of the concepts of mental act, awareness, image, abstract idea, and so on. Such analysis should be sufficient to dispel former problems involved in trying to introspect the answers to questions raised by Hume, Locke, and others.

But, oddly, Mace offers no evidence for saying flatly that the introspective facts are plainly there for all of us to see. He ignores arguments offered by others that it can be very difficult to "introspectively see" what is happening, even though the words and concepts available for description are readily enough understood. The opinion here is that Mace does not show that Locke and Berkeley differed about the existence of abstract ideas, because they did not understand the concept of an abstract idea or did not understand it in the same way; nor that the Würzburg school and Titchener disagreed about the existence of imageless thought, because they were conceptually muddled. The difficulty of grasping some of the concepts debated by philosophical psychologists, it can be argued, is the difficulty of being sure of the occasions when they are applicable. For example, distinctions exist between seeing an image, seeming to see an image, not seeming to see one, and not seeing one. My present experience, when introspected, may baffle me as to which of these concepts applies to it. The difference between two types of bacilli may be extremely difficult to detect under the microscope. It may take me a long time to *learn to*

see the difference. When I introspect, do I find imageless phenomena? Perhaps, if imageless phenomena occur, they ought
to be readily distinguishable from images, but they may be
extremely difficult to distinguish from the phenomena that I
report by saying that I *seem* to see images. It may take a long
time to learn to tell the difference. In summary, I can ask many
questions about my experiences that resist answering in terms
of what I am aware of and can introspect. Sometimes the
explanation for this may be, as Mace claims, that our questions
and concepts are confused though the "experience is clear
enough." But it does seem often the case that, though the
questions and concepts are not confused, the experience itself
does not yield readily to analysis. However, in time, they may
yield to the analytic philosopher who is introspectively sensitive
through having done some introspecting.

We have just now been talking about introspection as a
present paying attention to one's present states of mind, suggesting that it *is* relevant to the discussion of traditional
philosophical issues, suggesting that introspection cannot be
replaced wholesale by analysis of concepts. We argued in
Chapter Six that introspection of this sort is important, inasmuch as you tend to become what you repeatedly feel, for the
many-faceted task of self-control. We argued in Chapter Eight
that it is also important, as introspection of the "just past" and
thus not involving memory, for keeping the record of oneself
in the interest of self-knowledge. We used the studies of Bakan
and Singer in this chapter as arguments that introspection,
conceived as an activity of self-questioning, self-dialogue, and
self-analysis, as retrospective in employing memory, is indispensable for self-knowledge. All this contributes overwhelming
evidence against the assertion, commonly heard nowadays, that
we find out about ourselves in just the same ways that we make
discoveries about others. That assertion has been used to dis-
qualify introspection as important, whereas we have been
calling upon introspection to discredit the assertion.

Finally, being introspective tends to accompany being philosophical, so it is ironical that philosophers fail to appreciate

this fact about themselves in ignoring or denying the relevance of introspection to their professional activity. In writing about free will, the nature of mathematical concepts, the existence of God, and so on, philosophers often give the appearance of simply following a line of argument on a public problem. But in fact it is more often the case that a philosopher, if he is at all original, has made the problem peculiarly his own, both in terms of how he conceives it and how he resolves it. We dare to guess that philosophers rarely ask themselves, prior to publishing an article or book, Is the problem solved? They probably address themselves with questions like, Am I prepared to publish it? Am I confident that my distinctive thesis is defensible (arguable)? Have I overlooked any obvious objections? Have I said too little or too much? Ought I to sit on it for a few weeks? Have I said something that really matters, or am I playing a professional game? Have I been sincere or coy? Did I persist or quit when the argument faltered and the real difficulty emerged? Is my problem logical or psychological? Asking and answering questions like these fits the conception of introspection presented by Bakan and Singer. Noting that philosophizing has its introspective part reminds us also that, as Socrates said, philosophizing and knowing oneself can and ought to overlap.

10

Self-Knowledge

Many thinkers, who are on the side of reason, may find themselves, because remembering the sad facts of life, curbing an instinctive urge to embrace Plato's confidence in what knowledge can do. You are moved by what you know, Plato believed, and if you know what is good, you will then try to do it, and if you know what is bad, you will try to avoid it. Plato's kind of faith in the moving power of knowledge is probably what underlies the appeal of the injunction to "know thyself."

The trouble of course is that we all have met people possessing keen insight into themselves but who are powerless to employ such insight for their own benefit. Their drives overpower, but without obliterating, their reason. Yet it would clearly be a mistake not to see these as exceptional cases and not to appreciate Plato's statement of what knowledge can do. Everything being equal, self-knowledge can only be applauded. In obvious ways it is indispensable for preparedness, self-security, and self-control. You would only recommend in abnormal cases that people ought to live in ignorance of themselves.

Self-knowledge is clearly relevant also to self-evaluation. Knowing one's own perversities makes preserving self-esteem difficult. But, as the preceding chapters have recognized, coming to know oneself is also difficult. Introspection plays an important part, but it is fallible and often frustrating. Self-knowledge is nowadays constantly in doubt, because we have learned from psychoanalysis how deceptive the techniques of self-deception are. Hyperbolic concern for the possibility of self-deception leads some thinkers to the curious conclusion that knowledge of others is actually easier to come by than knowledge of ourselves, and that, accordingly, we ought to try to learn about ourselves just as we learn about others. But this is plausible if we attend only to a person's behavior and forget the relevance of his *experiences*. The mistake of supposing that knowledge of others is more assured than knowledge of ourselves, on the grounds that we allow only their behavior to count and thus avoid the subjective traps of self-delusion, is apparent once we recall that our knowledge of others certainly depends in part upon their testimony about what they experience. We necessarily consider their testimony about the nature of their experiences before deciding what it is that they intend, hope, desire, believe, suspect, regret, and so on. We must therefore rely upon the accuracy of their testimony as a piece of introspective self-diagnosis. It is simpler to know oneself. Admittedly, to achieve this you have to worry about the possibility of self-deception. But, in knowing the character of another, you have to worry about the possibility of his self-deception as well as yours. Insofar as knowledge is relevant to evaluation, it really is easier, in this respect, to pass judgment upon oneself than upon someone else.

Some evaluations, it should be noted, are more exclusively tested in terms of behavior than others. A person's performances are what determine you to judge him to be generous, brave, ambitious. But we should need to know the true nature of his experiences, besides his behavior, to know whether, in the full sense of the words, he is a person "of character," possesses "fortitude," is sensitive, sympathetic, and so on. In general, it is certainly not the case that we find it easier to be confident about such evaluations when we make them about others than about ourselves. For, again, we must worry both about the other person's susceptibility to self-deception in diagnosing his own experiences and about our own susceptibility to self-deception in accepting his testimony.

However, an individual can make the process of self-evaluation more difficult by adopting for himself more severe standards than he sets for others, and not necessarily because he is masochistic or guilt-ridden. His relation to himself, after all, is more complex and extensive than his relationship to any other person. Suppose I am trying to decide whether I am more courageous than cowardly, more sensitive than callous, more thoughtful than impulsive, and so on. I may find myself hesitating a long time before responding confidently to my own questions here, because I not only review my behavior and experience in the past but also try to anticipate how I might act and feel in a remarkable variety of hypothetical situations that come to mind. I may feel reasonably certain about how I would respond in some but not in all of the imagined circumstances. And the presence of any such uncertainty is naturally experienced as a hiatus in self-knowledge. If I were not troubled by such uncertainty, I might then be open to the charge of only taking a casual, irresponsible interest in myself. But I might, and justifiably so, relax my standards in judging whether you are more courageous than cowardly, etc. If, knowing how you behaved and felt in a few specific situations, I feel confident about how you would behave and feel in a few other critical situations, I make my judgment. I decide about you with reference to a comparatively restricted set of situations, whereas I decide about myself with reference to a comparatively unrestricted set of circumstances. It can be argued that this is as it should be. If I were to insist upon the same standards for others as for myself, that would be tantamount to trying to treat everyone met as if he were myself. The consequences of doing that would be disastrous in the extreme.

Another factor complicating self-evaluation is the wealth of subjective detail to be considered. I constantly live in my feelings, sensations, images, impulses, tendencies, conflicts, hopes, worries, intentions, resolutions, etc. Yours I only occasionally encounter. Insofar as these are relevant to the assessment of personality, I am content, in judging you, to allow the small sample of subjective detail known to me from your life to determine the verdict. But, in judging myself, the task of sorting and diagnosing is much more complex. And, again, if I did not make it such, I might be open to the accusation that the interest I take in myself is irresponsible. That I do not consult, to the same extent, the subjective details of your experiences is demanded by the fact that, to try to do so, I should be trying to treat you as myself. I can take a profound interest in you and treat you in some respects as I do myself. In doing so, I must allow you to make for yourself the task of self-evaluation as difficult as I make it for myself. I must allow you to do it in the way that only you can do it. We are forced, to keep life moving, to pass our quicker judgments upon each other. But the spirit in which we do this may be more considerate and tentative, if we remember, despite the advantage of his own information, how each person finds it slow going in arriving at a deserved judgment about himself.

Notes

CHAPTER I

[1] *Meditations on First Philosophy,* VI.

[2] *A Treatise of Human Nature,* Vol. I, Book I, Part IV. It should be noted that, whereas Hume saw the problem as trying to introspect a self that is the same through successive moments, we see it as trying to introspect a self as a "momentary cause."

[3] *Ibid.,* Vol. II, Appendix.

[4] Ross Stagner, *Psychology of Personality* (New York: McGraw–Hill, 1961) p. 185.

[5] As examples, see G. E. M. Anscombe, *Intention* (Ithaca, N.Y.: Cornell University Press, (1957), and A. I. Melden, *Free Action* (London: Routledge & Kegan Paul, 1961).

[6] Distinguished contemporary discussions of issues involved here include: Gilbert Ryle, *The Concept of Mind* (London: Hutchinson's University Library, 1949), Ludwig Wittgenstein, *Philosophical Investigations* (Oxford: Basil Blackwell & Mott, Ltd., 1953), P. F. Strawson, *Individuals* (London: Methuen & Co., Ltd., 1959), and A. J. Ayer, *The Concept of a Person* (London: Macmillan & Co., Ltd., 1964).

153

[7] *Ethics,* Pt. III, Prop. II. Note. Quoted, with interesting comments by Stuart Hampshire in his *Spinoza* (Plymouth, Great Britain: Latimer Trend & Co., Ltd., 1956), pp. 98–99.

[8] As examples, see Ruth Wylie, *The Self-Concept* (Lincoln: The University of Nebraska Press, 1961), Herbert Fingarette, *The Self in Transformation* (New York: Basic Books, Inc., 1963), and Edith Jacobson, *The Self and the Object World* (New York: International Universities Press, Inc., 1964).

[9] As examples, see Anna Freud, *The Ego and the Mechanism of Defense* (New York: International Universities Press, Inc., 1936), Heinz Hartmann, *Ego Psychology and The Problem of Adaptation* (New York: International Universities Press, Inc., 1958), and Heinz Hartmann, *Essays on Ego Psychology* (New York: International Universities Press, Inc., 1964).

[10] See, for relevant details, the remarkable book by Bruno Bettelheim, *The Empty Fortress; Infantile Autism and the Birth of the Self* (New York: The Free Press, 1967).

CHAPTER II

[1] *Meditations on First Philosophy,* VI.

[2] For a recent discussion that partly vindicates Descartes' choice of the pineal gland, see Richard J. Wurtman and Julius Axelrod, "The Pineal Gland," *Scientific American* (July, 1965), pp. 50–60.

[3] Philosophers tend not to discuss the concept of "mental energy." Because of its use in psychoanalytic literature, however, the concept needs philosophical treatment.

[4] The point is made by A. J. Ayer, *The Concept of a Person* (London: Macmillan & Co., Ltd., 1964), p. 80.

[5] For a discussion of this example, see J. Kim, "On the Psycho-physical Identity Theory," Part II, sec. 3, *American Philosophical Quarterly,* III, 3 (July, 1966), pp. 277–285.

[6] See, for example, A. J. Ayer, *Op. Cit.,* p. 68, and Norman Malcolm, "Behaviorism as a Philosophy," in T. W. Wann, ed., *Behaviorism and Phenomenology* (Chicago: The University of Chicago Press, 1964), p.

154. Also Kurt Baier, "Smart on Sensations," *Australasian Journal of Philosophy,* 40 (1962), pp. 64–65.

[7] For an excellent, detailed discussion of this issue, see Richard Rorty, "Mind–Body Identity, Privacy, and Categories" in Stuart Hampshire, ed., *Philosophy of Mind* (New York: Harper & Row, 1966), pp. 30–63.

[8] See, in particular, Roderick Chisholm, *Perceiving* (Ithaca: Cornell University Press, 1957), Chapter 11.

[9] *Ibid.,* p. 169.

[10] As examples, see A. J. Ayer, *Thinking and Meaning* (London: H. K. Lewis & Co., Ltd. 1947), and Gilbert Ryle, *The Concept of Mind* (London: Hutchinson's University Library, 1949).

[11] This point is made by Hilary Putnam, "Robots: Machines or Artifically created Life?" in Stuart Hampshire, ed., *Philosophy of Mind* (New York: Harper & Row, 1966), p. 70.

[12] Chisholm, *Op. Cit.,* p. 185.

[13] Important discussions of the identity hypothesis include U. T. Place, "Is Consciousness a Brain Process?" *British Journal of Psychology,* XLVII (1956); reprinted in V. C. Chappell, ed., *The Philosophy of Mind* (Englewood Cliffs, N.J.: Prentice–Hall, Inc., 1962), pp. 101–160.
And Herbert Feigl, "The 'Mental' and the 'Physical,'" in *Minnesota Studies in the Philosophy of Science,* Vol. II Minnesota Press (1958), pp. 370–497.
Also J. J. C. Smart, "Sensations and Brain Processes," in V. C. Chappell, ed., *Op. Cit.,* pp. 160–173.
And Wilfrid Sellars, "The Identity Approach to the Mind-Body Problem," in Stuart Hampshire, *Op. Cit.,* pp. 7–30.

[14] J. J. C. Smart, *Loc. Cit.,* pp. 163–164.

[15] Notice, considering this remark, that the identity hypothesis seems to depend, for its interest, upon initially accepting a philosophical contrast between the mental and the physical.

[16] Much of this discussion is based upon reports in *The New York Times,* 1968 (March 3, March 31, April 6, April 7, April 30, and May 14).

CHAPTER III

[1] *Man on His Nature,* second edition (Garden City, N.Y.: Anchor Books, Doubleday, 1953), pp. 244–245.

[2] For pertinent discussions of this issue, see U. T. Place, "Is Consciousness a Brain Process?" and J. J. C. Smart, "Sensations and Brain Processes," in V. C. Chappell, ed., *Op. Cit.*

[3] For more detailed discussions of this, see the contributions of A. J. Ayer and Gilbert Ryle to "The Physical Basis of Mind: A Philosophers' Symposium," in Peter Laslett, *The Physical Basis of Mind* (Oxford: Basil Blackwell, 1957), pp. 70–79.

[4] *Dilemmas* (Cambridge, England: The University Press, 1954), pp. 102 ff.

[5] "Experience," in V. C. Chappell, ed., *Op. Cit.,* pp. 23–49.

[6] "The Problem of Perception," in Robert J. Swartz, ed., *Perceiving, Sensing, and Knowing* (Garden City, N.Y.: Anchor Books, Doubleday, 1965), p. 506.

[7] William James often wrote as if he believed in the suggestiveness of this analogy. Perhaps H. H. Price also in *Thinking and Experience* (London: Hutchinson's University Library, 1953), p. 76.

[8] See, for instance, Charles W. Eriksen, "Discrimination and Learning without Awareness: A Methodological Survey and Evaluation," *The Psychological Review* (September, 1960), pp. 279–300.

[9] Based upon a report in *The New York Times,* June 13, 1968.

CHAPTER IV

[1] See Jean Matter Mandler and George Mandler, eds., *Thinking: From Association to Gestalt* (New York: John Wiley & Sons, Inc., 1964).

[2] *Thinking and Meaning* (London: H. K. Lewis & Co., Ltd., 1947).

[3] For a detailed account, see George Humphrey, *Thinking* (London: Methuen & Co., Ltd., 1951). Also E. G. Boring, "A History of Introspection," *The Psychological Bulletin* (1953), Vol. 50, pp. 169–189. Reprinted in E. G. Boring, *Psychologist at Large* (New York: Basic Books, 1961), pp. 210–246.

[4] Humphrey, *Op. Cit.*, p. 58.

[5] *Ibid.*

[6] *Ibid.*, p. 57.

[7] *Ibid.*, Chapter VIII.

[8] For example, see Gilbert Ryle, *The Concept of Mind* (London: Hutchinson's University Library, 1949), (2) in Chapter II.

[9] *Thought and Language* (Edited and Translated by Eugenia Hanfmann and Gertrude Vakar. Cambridge, Mass.: The M.I.T. Press, 1962).

[10] *Ibid.*, p. 18.

[11] *Ibid.*, pp. 138–139.

[12] *Ibid.*, p. 145.

[13] *Ibid.*, pp. 149–150.

[14] *Philosophical Investigations* (Oxford: Basil Blackwell & Mott, Ltd., 1953), especially #318–#361.

CHAPTER V

[1] Robert Ardrey, *African Genesis* (New York: Atheneum, 1961), *The Territorial Imperative* (New York: Atheneum, 1966).

Konrad Lorenz, *On Aggression* (New York: Harcourt, Brace & World, Inc., 1963).

Anthony Storr, *Human Aggression* (New York: Atheneum, 1968).

[2] This point made by Storr, *Op. Cit.*, p. 8.

[3] For a detailed discussion, see C. N. Cofer and M. H. Appley, *Motivation: Theory and Research* (New York: John Wiley & Sons, Inc., 1964), pp. 714 ff.

[4] J. D. Carthy and F. J. Ebling, editors and convenors, Institute of Biology Symposia, *The Natural History of Aggression*, No. 13, October, 1963 (London and New York: Academic Press, 1964), p. 3.

[5] It is also a thesis of Storr, *Op. Cit.*, who dedicates his book to Lorenz.

[6] S. A. Barnet, *Scientific American* (February, 1967), pp. 135–138.

[7] John Paul Scott, review article in *The Nation*, January 9, pp. 53–54, 1967.

[8] *Ibid.*, p. 53.

[9] *Ibid.*

[10] Cofer and Appley, *Op. Cit.*, p. 761. Our discussion is indebted to this work.

[11] See also Leonard Berkowitz, *Aggression; A Social Psychological Analysis*, (New York: McGraw–Hill, 1962), especially Chapter I.

[12] Reported in *The New York Times*, July 11, 1968.

[13] Alan E. Fisher, "Chemical Stimulation of the Brain," *Scientific American* (June, 1964), pp. 2–10.

[14] Barnet and Scott, *Loc. Cit.*, respectively.

[15] In following Lorenz, Storr as a psychotherapist adopts this "constructive" interpretation of aggression.

[16] Henry Block and Herbert Ginsburg, "The Psychology of Robots," *Psychology Today* (April, 1968), pp. 50–55. This is both instructive and entertaining reading.

[17] Ralph W. Gerard once expressed the idea somewhere in saying that, where there is a twisted thought, there must underlie it a twisted molecule.

[18] For helpful discussions of the philosophical concept of causality, see Sidney Morgenbesser's review article in *Scientific American* (February, 1961), pp. 175–178; and Ernest Nagel, "Some Notes on Determinism," in Sidney Hook, ed., *Determinism and Freedom in the Age of Modern Science* (New York: Collier Books, 1961), pp. 196–201.

[19] See, for instance, B. F. Skinner, "How To Teach Animals," *Scientific American* (December, 1951), pp. 2–5.

See also E. G. Boring, "When is Human Behavior Predetermined?" in his *Psychologist at Large* (New York: Basic Books, 1961). Boring says that his essay was prompted by B. F. Skinner's "propaganda" in his book *Science and Human Behavior* (1953) "for the universal belief of educated people (Harvard students) in the predetermination of human behavior."

Skinner is quoted as having said in 1959: "Pavlov had shown the way, and I could not then, as I cannot now, move without a jolt from ordinary reflexes to the important business of the organism in everyday life." (Quoted in Arthur J. Bachrach, ed., *Experimental Foundations of Clinical Psychology* (New York: Basic Books, 1962), p. 105.

[20] "Further recommendations in the Technique of Psycho-Analysis Recollection, Repetition and Working Through." *Collected Papers* (transl. by Riviere, Vol 2, New York: Basic Books, 1959), p. 369.

[21] "The 'Uncanny,'" Vol. 4, *Collected Papers,* Ibid., p. 391.

[22] See, for example, A. A. Brill, *Lectures on Psychoanalytic Psychiatry* (New York: Vintage Books, 1955), pp. 146–147.

Also: Helene Deutsch, *Neuroses and Character Types* (New York: International Universities Press, 1965), p. 75.

[23] See Donald H. Ford and Hugh B. Urban, *Systems of Psychotherapy* (New York: John Wiley & Sons, Inc., 1964), pp. 130–131.

[24] *Essay Concerning Human Understanding,* Bk. II, ch. XXI, 10. For thinking of this passage from Locke, I am indebted to a paper by Prof. Keith Lehrer read at a symposium at Oberlin College.

[25] An excellent philosophical study of our topic is by R. S. Peters, *The Concept of Motivation* (New York: Humanities Press, 1960).

An interesting group of essays relevant to one aspect of our topic is in Norman S. Greenfield and William C. Lewis, ed., *Psychoanalysis and Current Biological Thought* (Madison and Milwaukee: University of Wisconsin Press, 1965).

CHAPTER VI

[1] For further discussion of this, see D. O. Hebb, *The Organization of Behavior* (New York: John Wiley & Sons, Inc., 1949), Chapter 10.

Also: Robert Plutchik, *The Emotions* (New York: Random House, 1962), Chapter III.

[2] *The Principles of Psychology,* Vol. 2 (New York: Holt, 1890), Chapter XXV.

[3] For the opposed or "centralized" theory, see W. B. Cannon, *Bodily Changes in Pain, Hunger, Fear and Rage* (New York: Appleton, 1929).

[4] For further discussion of what is involved here, see Gilbert Ryle's chapter on "Emotion" in his *The Concept of Mind.* This is the source of many treatments of emotion in contemporary philosophical literature.

[5] Interesting discussions of the concept of the "unconscious" include A. C. MacIntyre, *The Unconscious* (London: Routledge & Kegan Paul, Ltd., 1958).
And R. S. Peters, *The Concept of Motivation,* Chapter Three. (New York: Humanities Press, 1958).
Also: Abraham Edel, "The Concept of the Unconscious: Some Analytic Preliminaries," *Philosophy of Science,* Vol. 31, No. 1 (January, 1964), pp. 18–33.
Also: Harvey Mullane, "Unconscious Emotion," *Theoria,* Vol. XXXI, 3; 1965, pp. 181–190.

[6] See Plutchik, *Op. Cit.,* p. 32.
See also David Rapaport, *Emotions and Memory* (New York: Science Editions, Inc., 1961), pp. 28 ff.

[7] For examples, see Rollo May, ed., *Existence: A New Dimension in Psychiatry and Psychology* (New York: Basic Books, Inc., 1958).
Also: Medard Boss, *Psychoanalysis and Daseinsanalysis* (New York: Basic Books, Inc., 1963).

[8] See Plutchik, *Op. Cit.,* pp. 50 ff.

[9] *Ibid.,* p. 151.

[10] For an interesting discussion of empathy, see Edith Stein, *On the Problem of Empathy* (The Hague: Martinus Nijhoff, 1964).

[11] See Plutchik, *Op. Cit.,* for more on this. Plutchik, incidentally, remains in this tradition.

[12] See Plutchik, p. 42.

[13] Compare Anthony Kenny, *Action, Emotion, and Will* (London: Routledge & Kegan Paul, 1963), p. 55.

[14] T.L.V., in "Molecular Biology and the Division in Man" (*The Listener,* 25 April 1968, pp. 532–535), argues in an interesting way for the thesis that Western tradition "trains our intellects but fails to educate our feelings."

[15] For further discussion of issues raised here, see Gerald E. Myers, "Motives and Wants," *Mind* (April, 1964), pp. 173–185; and "Feelings Into Words," *The Journal of Philosophy* (December 19, 1963), pp. 801–811.

Also: T. F. Daveney, "Feelings, Causes and Mr. Myers," *Mind* (October, 1967), pp. 592–594.

CHAPTER VII

[1] Ludwig Wittgenstein's later philosophy, it has seemed to many including myself (though Norman Malcolm has cautioned against this interpretation), brings out the "psychoanalytic" nature of certain philosophical problems, arguments, and positions.

[2] Important examples from the literature include:

Sir Henry Head, *Studies in Neurology,* Vol 2, (London: Oxford, 1920); and *Aphasia and kindred disorders of speech* (London: Cambridge, 1926).

Paul Schilder, *The image and appearance of the human body* (London: Kegan Paul Trench, Trubner & Co., 1935).

S. F. Fisher and S. E. Cleveland, *Body image and personality* (Princeton: Van Nostrand, 1958).

M. Merleau-Ponty, *Phenomenology of Perception* (London: Routledge, 1962).

Seymour Wapner and Heinz Werner, *The Body Percept* (New York: Random House, 1965).

[3] These remarks are based upon several years of collaborating with my wife, Martha Myers, who has choreographed and taught dance at Smith College and Connecticut College.

[4] Seymour Fisher and Sidney E. Cleveland, "Personality, Body Perception, and Body Image Boundary," in Wapner and Werner, *Op. Cit.,* p. 51. Much of this discussion is indebted to this essay.

[5] Macdonald Critchley, "Disorders of Corporeal Awareness in Parietal Disease," in Wapner and Werner, *Op. Cit.,* p. 74. We are indebted to this essay for other information mentioned.

[6] Fisher and Cleveland, *Loc. Cit.*, p. 53.

[7] William E. Henry, *The Analysis of Fantasy* (New York: John Wiley & Sons, Inc., 1956), p. 26.

[8] William Braden, *The Private Sea: LSD & The Search for God* (New York: Bantam Books, Inc., 1967), p. 193.

[9] Robert S. De Ropp, *Drugs and the Mind* (New York: Grove Press, Inc., 1961), p. 52.

[10] An excellent discussion in behalf of this general thesis is B.A.O. Williams, "Personal Identity and Individuation," in Donald F. Gustafson, *Essays in Philosophical Psychology* (Garden City, N.Y.: Anchor Books, Doubleday, 1964), pp. 324–346.

Wittgenstein was apparently making a similar point in remarking that the best picture of the human soul is the human body *(Philosophical Investigations,* II, IV.)

[11] This was not a point that Aldous Huxley, for example, was prepared to grant—or so it seemed, in discussions had with him not long before his death.

For other remarks on this topic, see Gerald E. Myers, "Self and Body-Image," in James M. Edie, ed., *Phenomenology in America* (Chicago: Quadrangle Books, 1967), pp. 147–161.

CHAPTER VIII

[1] "Memory," *The Listener* (May 2, 1968), pp. 571–573.

[2] *Ibid.,* p. 572.

[3] For readable accounts of this, see David Perlman, "The Search for the Memory Molecule," *The New York Times Magazine,* July 7, 1968.

Also: "Evolving Molecular Theories of Memory and RNA," *Roche Report, Frontiers of Clinical Psychiatry,* January 15, 1966.

[4] *The Roche Report* (above)

[5] See J. Anthony Deutsch, "Neural basis of Memory," *Psychology Today,* Vol. 1, No. 12 (May, 1968), p. 61.

[6] *Ibid.*

[7] Ralph W. Gerard, "What is Memory?" *Scientific American* (September, 1953), p. 3.

[8] John Ceraso, "The Interference Theory of Forgetting," *Scientific American* (October, 1967), p. 124.

[9] A. R. Luria, *The Mind of a Mnemonist,* transl. by Lynn Solotaroff (New York: Basic Books, Inc., 1968).

[10] *Ibid.,* pp. 22–23.

[11] *Ibid.,* p. 159.

[12] See, for example, Ernest G. Schachtel, "On Memory and Childhood Amnesia," in Clara Thompson, ed., *An Outline of Psychoanalysis,* revised edition (New York: Modern Library, 1955), pp. 203–227.

[13] See David Rapaport, *Emotion and Memory* (New York: Science Editions, Inc., 1961).

[14] The researcher is Dr. Jules Hirsh of The Rockefeller University, an interesting interview with whom is reported by Jane E. Brody in *The New York Times* of October 17, 1968.

[15] For a criticism of this notion, see A. J. Ayer, *The Problem of Knowledge* (Edinburg: A Pelican Book, 1956), Chapter 4.

[16] See W. Von Leyden, *Remembering; A Philosophical Problem* (London: Gerald Duckworth & Co., Ltd., 1961), Chapter X.

[17] *Ibid.,* p. 78.

[18] Both Gilbert Ryle, in his *The Concept of Mind,* and Von Leyden, in his *Remembering,* recognize this use of "to remember."

[19] Von Leyden, Chapter VI.

[20] Ryle, *The Concept of Mind,* pp. 163–167. William James accepted this also in his psychological writings.

[21] Ayer, *Op. Cit.,* p. 152.

[22] This idea is emphasized by Charles Hartshorne in "Mind as Memory and Creative Love," in Jordan M. Scher, ed., *Theories of the Mind* (New York: The Free Press of Glencoe, 1962), pp. 440–464.

[23] Wittgenstein: "When I see the picture of a galloping horse . . . is it superstition to think I *see* the horse galloping in the picture?— And does my visual impression gallop too?" *Philosophical Investigations,* p. 202.

CHAPTER IX

[1] William James, *The Principles of Psychology,* Vol. 2 (New York: Holt, 1890), p. 185.

[2] Quoted by E. B. Titchener, "Prolegomena to a Study of Introspection," *American Journal of Psychology,* 23:427–48 (July, 1912), p. 443.

[3] See C. A. Mace, "Introspection and Analysis," in Max Black, ed., *Philosophical Analysis* (Ithaca: Cornell University Press, 1950), p. 235.

[4] See E. G. Boring, "A History of Introspection," in E. G. Boring, *Psychologist at Large* (New York: Basic Books, 1961).

[5] For more on this difference between James and Brentano, see William James, *Loc. Cit.* Vol. 1, p. 189.

[6] Boring, *Loc. Cit.,* p. 224.

[7] For differing views on this, see Ledger Wood, "Inspection and Introspection," *Philosophy of Science.* 7:220–228, 1940, and Peter McKellar, "The Method of Introspection," in Jordan Scher, ed., *Theories of the Mind* (New York: The Free Press of Glencoe, 1962) pp. 619–645.

[8] "A Reconsideration of the Problem of Introspection," reprinted in Bakan, *On Method; Toward a Reconstruction of Psychological Investigation* (San Francisco, Jossey–Bass Inc., 1968), pp. 94–113. See also in same work Chapter 10. "Suicide and The Method of Introspection," pp. 113–122.

[9] Jerome L. Singer, *Daydreaming; An Introduction to the Experimental Study of Inner Experience* (New York: Random House, 1966).

[10] *Ibid.,* p. xv.

[11] *Ibid.,* p. 28.

[12] *Ibid.,* pp. 28–29.

[13] Quoted by Singer, *Ibid.,* p. 81.

[14] For other examples of recent introspective studies, see McKellar, *Loc. Cit.*

[15] "The sorts of things that I can find out about myself are the same as the sorts of things that I can find out about other people, and the methods of finding them out are much the same." Gilbert Ryle, *The Concept of Mind,* p. 155

[16] Quoted by Alan R. White, *The Philosophy of Mind* (New York: Random House, 1967), p. 99.

[17] C. A. Mace *Loc. Cit.,* p. 238.

[18] *Ibid.,* p. 236.

Supplementary
Bibliography

Allport, Gordon, *The Person in Psychology* (Boston: Beacon Press, 1968).

Anderson, Alan Ross, ed., *Minds and Machines* (Englewood Cliffs, N.J.: Prentice-Hall, Inc., 1964).

Armstrong, D. M., *Bodily Sensations* (London: Routledge & Kegan Paul, 1962).

Bartlett, Sir Frederic, *Thinking* (New York: Basic Books, 1958).

Bruner, J. S., Goodnow, J. J., & Austin, G. A., *A Study of Thinking* (New York: John Wiley & Sons, Inc., 1956).

Bruner, J. S., Oliver, R. R., & Greenfield, P. M., *et al., Studies in Cognitive Growth* (New York: John Wiley & Sons, Inc., 1966).

Crosson, F. J., & Sayre, K. M., eds., *The Modelling of Mind* (South Bend: University of Notre Dame Press, 1963).

Flew, Antony, ed., *Body, Mind, and Death* (New York: The Macmillan Company, 1964).

Flugel, J. C., *Studies in Feeling and Desire* (London: Gerald Duckworth & Co., Ltd., 1955).

Geach, Peter, *Mental Acts* (London: Routledge & Kegan Paul, Ltd., 1957).

Hampshire, Stuart, *Thought and Action* (London: Chatto and Windus, Ltd., 1959).

Hook, Sidney, ed., *Psychoanalysis, Scientific Method and Psychology* (Washington Square: New York University Press, 1959).

——, *Dimensions of Mind* (New York: Collier Books, 1961).

Norbeck, E., Price-Williams, & McCord, W., *The Study of Personality* (New York: Holt, Rinehart and Winston, Inc., 1968).

Russell, Bertrand, *The Analysis of Mind* (London: George Allen & Unwin, Ltd., 1921).

Shoemaker, Sydney, *Self-Knowledge and Self-Identity* (Ithaca: Cornell University Press, 1963).

Vinacke, W. E., *The Psychology of Thinking* (New York: McGraw-Hill, Inc., 1952).

Index

acetycholine, 72
achievement, 49
acids, 71–72
   See also names of acids
action
   as causal process, 26
   children as operating upon their environment, 28
   as free, 79–80
   momentary cause of, 25–27
aggression, 75–78
   frustration and, 75
   as an instinct, 75–76, 78
amino acid, 71
amputees, 15
anger, 76, 89, 91, 92, 94
angina pectoris, 43
anxiety, 36, 92
   from daydreams, 140
Aristotle, 48, 61, 89, 96, 144
autistic children, 27–28
autosuggestion, 155
Ayer, A. J., 60–61, 124–125

Bakan, David, 136–139, 144, 146, 147
barrier score, 108
behavior
   emotion and, 90
   experience and, 50, 51
   Freud on, 83–84
   operant, 82
   respondent, 51, 82

behaviorism, 36–38, 132, 135
belief, 35–38
Berkeley, George, 144, 145
Berkowitz, Leonard, 77
Beyond the Pleasure Principle (Freud), 84
Bible, the, on the self, 18–19
biology, memory and, 116–119
biophysics, experience and, 45–48
body, human, 29–44
   common concept of, 24
   philosophy on, 31–32
   the self and, 14–17, 24
   substituting the word "organism" for, 24–25
   theory of dualism, 29–31
body-boundary, 108–109
body-image
   changes in, 107–108
   distortions and oddities, 110
   fantasies and, 105–115
   obesity and, 122
   the self and, 109–115
brain, the, 30
   changes in body-image and, 107–108
   experience and, 45–48
   the identity hypothesis, 38–41
   increasing size of, 74
   radio stimulation of, 73
Brentano, Franz, 133

cardiovascular diseases, 44
Cartesianism, 29–31

catharsis, 89
cause, 26, 42–44
    domino theory of, 80–81
    mental properties of, 30
    in motivation, 79–87
Ceraso, John, 119, 120
childhood, daydreams from, 139–141
children
    autistic, 27–28
    as causally operating upon their environment, 28
    egocentric speech, 66–68
    egocentric thought, 66–67
    as striving and demanding organisms, 28
    use of "I," 23, 27–28
clairvoyance, 34
Cleveland, Sidney, 108
computers, 74
Creutzfeld-Jakob disease, 72

Darwin, Charles, 63, 90
Daydreaming (Singer), 142
daydreams, 139–142
    anxiety from, 140
    from childhood, 139–141
    ethnic groups, 142
death instinct, 75
decision, 84–86
    forced, 84–85
    motivation and, 82–87
déjà vu (experience), 48
Delgado, J. M. R., 73
depression, 44
Descartes, René, 16, 29–31, 59, 60, 100, 102–103, 116
Deutsch, Anthony, 118
diet, 72, 122
discriminating, 49–50
displacement, 31
dizziness, 94, 95
DNA (deoxyribonucleic acid), 71
domino theory of causality, 80–81
Dostoyevsky, Fyodor, 95
dreams, 31, 57, 136, 139–142
drugs, 112–114, 115
    memory and, 117, 118
    See also names of drugs
dualism, 29–31
    philosophical fantasy of, 110–112, 115
Dürr, E., 62

ego, 17, 31
egocentric speech, 66–68
egocentric thinking, 66–68

eidetic memory, 120
electroencephalograph, 74
emotions, 88–101
    behavior and, 90
    as disorganized responses, 90
    distinguished from feelings, 93–96
    personality and, 90
    self-deception about, 91–92
    theories of, 88–93
Existentialists, 93
experience, 45–58
    behavior and, 50, 51
    biophysics and, 45–48
    the brain and, 45–48
    co-awareness of, 47
    Farrell on, 49–52
    motivation and, 81–82
    as objects, 54
    particular, 54–58
    perceiving as, 48–54
    puzzling aspect of, 45
    Quinton on, 52–53
    Ryle on, 48–52
    Sherrington on, 45–47, 49
    temporal boundaries, 55–56
    thought and, 60
    unconscious awareness in, 56–57
Experimentalists, 77–78
evolution, chemical, 71
eye movement, 58

fantasies, 102–115, 139–142
    body-image and, 105–115
    mild, 104
    philosophical, of dualism, 110–112
    psychotic, 104
    severe, 104
Farrell, B. A., 49–52
fate neurotic, 83
fear, 38–41, 90, 91, 94, 100
feelings, 31, 88–100, 136
    distinguished from emotions, 93–96
    knowing, 96–101
    most important fact about, 96
    theories of, 88–93
Fisher, Seymour, 108
forgetting, 119–120, 122
    decay theory of, 119
    interference theory of, 119
free association, 121
Freud, Sigmund, 30–31, 75, 83–84, 93, 141, 142
Freudianism, 30–31, 135–136
frustration, aggression and, 75

Gerard, R. W., 118–119
Gestalt psychology, 133, 134
"giving up," 44
globulin, 43
glyoprotein neuramic acid, 73
guilt, 78, 136–137

habits, 81
hallucinations, 31, 42, 104
Harlow, H. F., 76
Harvard Medical School, 72
hate, 92, 100
Head, Sir Henry, 105
hearing, 45–47, 52–53, 56–57
    memory and, 127–128
Hebb, D. O., 88
histamine, 73
Hobbes, Thomas, 100
Holtzman test, 108
hormones, 71, 73
Hume, David, 17–18, 19, 20, 22, 23, 25,
    27, 145
Humphrey, George, 63, 64
hunger, 76
hypnosis, 121

"I," 14–16, 20–23
    children's use of, 23, 27–28
    Hume on, 17–18
    as a momentary cause, 25–27
    the word "organism" and, 24–25
id, 31
identity hypothesis, 38–41
imagination, 102–103, 114
impersonal pronouns, 14
ink blot series, 108–109
inner speech, 65–69
instinct
    aggression as, 75–76, 78
    repetition-compulsion as, 83
Instinctualists, 77–78
intentionality, 35–38
introspection, 124, 131–147
    Bakan on, 136–139, 144, 145, 147
    concepts of, 131–136
    phenomenological, 134
    Mace on, 144–146
    philosophy and, 142–147
    recent studies, 136–142
    scientific, 133
    as self-analysis, 136
    Singer on, 139–142, 144, 145, 147
    as a source of knowledge, 131–133
I.Q., 43, 72

James, William, 77, 86, 90, 91, 124–
    125, 132, 133
jealousy, 91, 92

Kant, Immanuel, 131, 132
knee jerk reflex, 44
knowledge, 21–23
    experiencing one's self and, 27
    introspection as a source of, 131–133
    self-, 17–18, 27, 130, 148–151
Külpe, O., 62

Locke, John, 85, 86, 144, 145
Lorenz, Konrad, 75–77, 78
Love, 100
LSD, 19, 112–113
Luria, A. R., 120–121

McDougall, William, 100
Mace, C. A., 144–146
man, earliest ancestors of, 71
Massachusetts Institute of Technology,
    74, 75
memory, 72, 116–130
    biology and, 116–119
    drugs and, 117, 118
    due to self-interest, 130
    as egoistic, 129
    eidetic, 120
    hearing and, 127–128
    long-term, 116–117
    obesity and, 122
    personality and, 121–122
    philosophy and, 122–124
    primary function of, 125
    psychology and, 119–122
    retrospection and, 124–128
    seeing and, 127–128
    the self and, 128–130
    sensitization, 116, 117
    short-term, 116, 117
    three forms of, 116
memory molecule, 118
memory pill, 118
mental retardation, 73
mental science, psychology as, 29
mental states, 36–38
    the identity hypothesis, 38–41
mescaline, 110–111
Metrazol, 118
Mill, John Stuart, 86
mind, 29–44
    autonomy of reports of, 34–35
    causal properties of, 30

intentionality, 35–38
philosophy on, 31–32
psychoanalytic theory, 30–31
the self and, 16–17
theory of dualism, 29–31
Mind of a Mnemonist, The (Luria), 120–121
"Moral Equivalent of War, The" (James), 77
motion, 31–32
motivation, 70–87
aggression, 75–78
cause and, 79–87
contemporary research, 70–75
decision and, 82–87
experiences and, 81–82
Motivational theory, 90
"myself," 14–16
Hume on, 17–18

naked thought, 61–65
nonbodily something, the self as, 16–17

obesity, 122
On Aggression (Lorenz), 75–77
"oneself," 14–16
operant behavior, 82
organisms, 25–27
children as, 28
meaning of, 24
as mental, 29–44
as physical, 29–44
substituting the word for "body," 24–25
Organization of Behavior (Hebb), 88

pain, 43, 59, 124
particular experiences, 54–58
Pauling, Linus, 72
perceiving as experiencing, 48–54
personal pronouns, 14–18, 20–28
personality
emotion and, 90
memory and, 121–122
Phaedo (Plato), 13
phenomenological description, 134
philosophical dualism, 29–31, 110–112, 115
philosophy
concept of the self, 14–23
introspection and, 142–147
memory and, 122–124
mental and physical events, 31–32
thought and, 64
physical events, 29–44
contrast of mental and physical, 41–44

intentionality, 35–38
the identity hypothesis, 38–41
Piaget, Jean, 66
pineal gland, 30
Plato, 13, 39, 47, 102, 148
poetry, 43
preconscious, 31
pronouns, 28
impersonal, 14
personal, 14–18, 20–28
proteins, 72, 73
Proust, Marcel, 141
psychoanalytic theory, 30–31, 135–136
biological orientation of, 31
psychology
Gestalt, 133, 134
importance of the self, 27
memory and, 119–122
as the mental science, 29
Würzburg, 61–64, 68, 133, 145
pursuing fate, 83

quantum mechanics, 33
Quinton, A. M., 52–53

remorse, 100
repetition-compulsion, principle of, 83–84
repression, 31, 121
resentment, 92
respondent behavior, 51, 82
retrospection, 129, 133
memory and, 124–128
primary function of, 125
RNA (ribonucleic acid), 71–72, 87, 117, 118
Rorschach test, 108
Russell, Bertrand, 103
Ryle, Gilbert, 48–52, 142

Sartre, Jean-Paul, 96
schizophrenia, 43, 48, 73, 108
science, concept of the self and, 20
seeing, 45–47, 54–58
as experiencing, 48–54
eye movement and, 58
memory and, 127–128
self, 13–28
Biblical reference to, 18–19
body-image and, 109–115
the human body and, 14–17, 24
Hume on, 17–18, 19, 20, 22, 23, 25, 27
importance in clinical psychology, 27
memory and, 128–130
the mind and, 16–17
as a momentary cause, 25–27

as a nonbodily something, 16–17
philosophical concept of, 14–23
as a primitive experience, 18–19
Socrates on, 13, 14, 15, 20, 23
as an unscientific concept, 20
self-analysis, 136
self-deception, 91–92, 149–150
self-evaluation, 149–151
self-knowledge, 17–18, 27, 130, 148–141
self-evaluation and, 148–151
sensitization, 116, 117
set, 36–37
Sherrington, Sir Charles, 45–47, 49
Singer, Jerome, 139–142, 144, 146, 147
Skinner, B. F., 82–83
sleep, 71
smelling, 52, 56, 57
Socrates, 13, 14, 15, 20, 23, 39, 147
sorrow, 32, 33–35, 100
soul, 17, 30
speech
    egocentric, 66–68
    inner, 65–69
    overt, 68
Spinoza, Baruch, 24, 100
staring, 48–49
strychnine, 118
superego, 31
superscientific instruments, 34, 35
symbols, thought and, 60–61

tasting, 52, 57
telepathy, 34
tendency, 81
things, 29–30
thought, 59–69
    Aristotle on, 61
    Ayer on, 60–61
    egocentric, 66–68

experience and, 60
Humphrey on, 63, 64
inner speech, 65–69
naked, 61–65
philosophy and, 64
Piaget on, 66
process of, 59–61
specialized concepts of, 60
symbols and, 60–61
Titchener on, 62, 64
Vygotsky on, 66–68
Wittgenstein on, 69
words and, 64–65
Wundt on, 61–62
thyroxin, 73
Titchener, E. B., 62, 64, 132–133, 145
touching, 52, 57
transference, 31
unconscious, 31
unconscious awareness, 56–57
University of California, 74
uric acid, 72

vanity, 91
verbs, 49, 50
viruses, 71, 72
vitamins, 72
Vygotsky, Lev S., 66–68

Wells, Martin, 116, 117
Wertheimer, Max, 134
Western Reserve University, 74
Wittgenstein, Ludwig, 69, 142–143
Wundt, Wilhelm, 61–62, 132–133
Würzburg psychologists, 61–64, 68, 133, 145

Xantippe, 39

Yale University, 73, 75